Availability
Management

IT Infrastructure Library

CCTA

Central Computer and Telecommunications Agency

LONDON: THE STATIONERY OFFICE

This is one of the books in the IT Infrastructure
Library series.

For further information on CCTA products,
contact:

CCTA Library,
Rosebery Court,
St Andrews Business Park
NORWICH NR7 0HS.
Telephone 01603 704930
GTN 3040 4930

This document has been produced using
procedures conforming to
BS 5750 Part 1: 1987; ISO 9001: 1987.

Table of contents

1.	**Management summary**	**1**
1.1	Background	1
1.2	IT service failures	1
1.3	What is needed	2
1.4	Benefits	3
1.5	About this module	3
2.	**Introduction**	**5**
2.1	Purpose	5
2.2	Target readership	6
2.3	Scope	6
2.4	Related guidance	8
2.5	Standards	10
3.	**Planning for availability management**	**13**
3.0	Concepts	13
3.0.1	Terminology	14
3.0.2	Security	15
3.0.3	Availability management process	18
3.0.4	Designing for availability	21
3.1	Procedures	23
3.1.1	Feasibility Study	24
3.1.2	Agree objectives and scope	26
3.1.3	Mount an availability awareness exercise	27
3.1.4	Initiate systems analysis	27
3.1.5	Analyze availability requirements	28
3.1.6	Data collection detail level	29
3.1.7	Analyze sources of actual availability data	30
3.1.8	Availability management data storage	33
3.1.9	Plan monitoring of availability	35
3.1.10	Plan reporting	36
3.1.11	Verify ability to meet requirements	37
3.1.12	The Availability Plan	39
3.1.13	Management reviews and audits	40
3.2	Dependencies	40
3.3	People	42
3.3.1	Availability Manager	42
3.3.2	Availability management section	43
3.4	Timing	44

4.   **Implementation**   **45**

4.1   Procedures and automated systems   45
4.1.1   Procedures   45
4.1.2   Support tools   48
4.2   Dependencies   50
4.3   People   50
4.4   Timing   50

5.   **Post-implementation and audit**   **51**

5.1   Procedures   51
5.1.1   Post-implementation review   51
5.1.2   Ongoing operation and review   53
5.1.3   Producing the Availability Plan   54
5.1.4   Review for efficiency and effectiveness   55
5.1.5   Auditing for compliance   57
5.2   Dependencies   58
5.3   People   59
5.4   Timing   59

6.   **Benefits, costs and possible problems**   **61**

6.1   Benefits   61
6.2   Costs   62
6.3   Possible problems   63

7.   **Tools**   **65**

7.1   Types of tools   65
7.1.1   Failure data recording   65
7.1.2   Databases   66
7.1.3   Report generation and statistical analysis   66
7.1.4   Modelling tools   67
7.1.5   Word processing and graphic presentation software   67
7.2   Tool selection   67
7.3   Interface requirements   68
7.4   Current tools   68
7.5   Advantages and pitfalls   68

8.   **Bibliography**   **71**

Annexes

A.	**Glossary of Terms**	**A1**
B.	**Methods for calculating availability**	**B1**
B.1	Introduction	B1
B.2	Formulae	B2
B.3	Example 1 - A simple infrastructure	B3
B.4	Example 2 - A larger infrastructure	B7
B.5	Conclusion	B10
C.	**Example job description - Availability Manager**	**C1**
D.	**Determining availability requirements**	**D1**
D.1	Defining downtime	D2
D.2	Specifying service hours	D3
D.3	Availability metrics	D3
E.	**Availability and incidents**	**E1**
F.	**Techniques for analyzing availability**	**F1**
F.1	Component Failure Impact Analysis	F1
F.2	Fault Tree Analysis	F2
G.	**Designing for availability**	**G1**
G.1	Outline design process	G1
G.2	Service design availability analysis	G1
G.3	Improving the design	G2
G.4	Central hardware	G3
G.5	Local hardware	G6
G.6	Networks	G8
G.7	Environment	G10
G.8	System software	G14
G.9	Application software and data	G15
G.10	Operational standards, procedures and training	G17
G.11	Contracts with suppliers	G19
H.	**Data items to be recorded for each incident**	**H1**

Foreword

Welcome to the IT Infrastructure Library module on **Availability Management** .

In their respective areas the IT Infrastructure Library publications complement and provide more detail than the IS Guides.

The ethos behind the development of the IT Infrastructure Library is the recognition that organizations are becoming increasingly dependent on IT in order to satisfy their corporate aims and meet their business needs. This growing dependency leads to growing requirement for quality IT services. In this context quality means 'matched to business needs and user requirements as these evolve'.

This module is one of a series of codes of practice intended to facilitate the quality management of IT services and of the IT Infrastructure. (By IT Infrastructure, we mean organizations' computers and networks - hardware, software and computer related communications, upon which application systems and IT services are built and run). The codes of practice will assist organizations to provide quality IT services in the face of skill shortages, system complexity, rapid change, growing user expectations, current and future user requirements.

Underpinning the IT Infrastructure is the Environmental Infrastructure upon which it is built. Environmental topics are covered in separate sets of guides within the IT Infrastructure Library.

IT infrastructure management is a complex subject which for presentational and practical reasons has been broken down within the IT Infrastructure Library into a series of modules. A complete list of current and planned modules is available from the CCTA IT Infrastructure Management Services at the address given at the back of this module.

The structure of the module is, in essence:

* a **Management summary** aimed at senior managers (Directors of IT and above, typically down to Civil Service Grade 5), senior IT staff and, in some cases, users or office managers (typically Civil Service Grades 5 to 7)

* the main body of the text, aimed at IT middle management (typically grades 7 to HEO)

* technical detail in Annexes.

The module gives the main **guidance** in sections 3 to 5; explains the **benefits, costs and possible problems** in section 6, which may be of interest to senior staff; and provides information on **tools** (requirements and examples of real-life availability) in section 7.

CCTA is working with the IT industry to foster the development of software tools to underpin the guidance contained within the codes of practice (ie to make adherence to the module more practicable), and ultimately to automate functions.

If you have any comments on this or other modules, do please let us know. A **Comments sheet** is provided with every module. Alternatively you may wish to contact us directly using the reference point given in **Further information**.

Thank you. We hope you find this module useful.

Acknowledgements

The assistance of the following contributors is gratefully acknowledged.

Bertel Aukema and Rene van't Veen (under contract to CCTA from Pink Elephant BV); Mr Aukema now works for Quint Wellington Redwood BV.

1. Management summary

1.1 Background

A recent European Commission survey suggested that one in five companies would be unable to function for more than a few hours in the event of a major computer breakdown causing the loss of IT services. Many financial institutions and travel organizations have become completely dependent on effective IT to run their businesses and would suffer damage to their business resulting from even a short breakdown. Some government departments are now, or soon will be, in a similar position. IT services must therefore be designed and maintained to manage risks to IT service provision.

This module concentrates on the serviceability, reliability, maintainability and resilience aspects of availability: there are, however, wider implications in security terms. Availability may be compromised by:

* staff shortage (eg strikes, lack of expertise)

* theft

* abuse of IT systems (leading to degradation of IT systems)

* vandalism.

CCTA publishes guidance to assist with security of IT systems and it is recommended that government organizations refer to the IT Security Library for further guidance. All organizations can refer to IS Guide C4 of the CCTA Information Systems Guides and to the CCTA Risk Analysis and Management Method (CRAMM) guides. Organizations are strongly advised to obtain a comprehensive view of potential risks to the IT installation or IT systems by undertaking a formal review of security using CRAMM.

1.2 IT service failures

Attention has focused in the past on hardware as being the least reliable component of the IT infrastructure. However, today's central processors are very much more reliable than those of even five years ago. A recent survey of installations in central government showed the main contributions to failure to be made up as shown in Figure 1, overleaf.

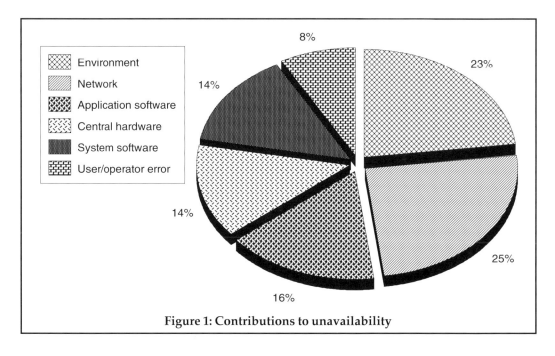

Figure 1: Contributions to unavailability

Figure 1 illustrates that effort needs to be directed at other elements of the IT infrastructure. In particular, networks and the environment are areas in need of attention. The greatest opportunity to specify and build high-availability IT services exists at the planning and design stages, before the component parts are developed, procured and assembled.

The availability of IT services depends on all the components illustrated by the pie chart. Ideally, there should be contracts with suppliers covering the availability requirements of all the components of the IT infrastructure. In practice it is not usually possible to cover every aspect of availability with contractual provision or stipulations.

1.3   What is needed

Availability management necessitates procedures to be put in place which are documented and practised - for example to track and deal with problem hardware or software; to ensure that customer requirements continue to be met; and to monitor conformance to contracts by suppliers. All relevant staff need to be aware of the existence of these procedures and the need for them. Effective problem and change management functions can be major contributors to high availability. Reference is made in this module to these and other IT Infrastructure Library modules as appropriate.

1.4 Benefits

Introducing availability management will assist an organization in the implementation of security policies to protect and provide quality IT services to customers. Customers will perceive an improvement in service quality, fewer disruptions to the IT services and more rapid recovery when services are disrupted.

1.5 About this module

This module provides guidance to organizations on how to achieve and sustain the IT service availability which customers need to support their business at a justifiable cost. The module focuses on the procedures and systems, including specification and monitoring of suppliers contractual obligations regarding availability, required to support availability requirements in Service Level Agreements.

Significantly, those organizations practising availability management have discovered that the cost of introducing the function is more than offset when compared to the cost to the business of IT services' downtime. IT Directorates necessarily are looking to satisfy customers and to play their part in helping the businesses of the organization to increase their efficiency and in turn satisfy their own customers.

Availability management is one of the most effective means of improving the quality of IT service delivered to customers. Availability management need not be created as a unique function; there is commonality particularly with capacity management and contingency planning that would enable an organization to introduce availability management functions in tandem with another related infrastructure management discipline.

2. Introduction

2.1 Purpose

The purpose of the module is to provide guidance to those responsible for, and concerned with, the availability aspects of IT services for as long as the services are required, through the full lifecycle of the project from feasibility studies, through to ongoing live operations and finally decommissioning.

Organizations rely more and more on IT services. As time passes, customers' dependency on IT becomes so great that:

* reversion to manual systems is not practical

* effectiveness and efficiency of the customers of IT services is strongly influenced by the availability of IT services

* business customers rely on IT to support business functions - without which an organization could not operate.

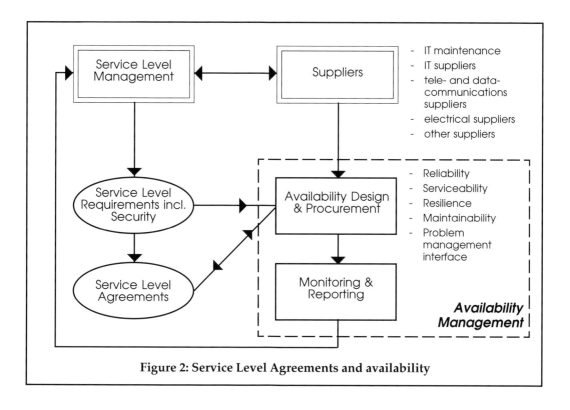

Figure 2: Service Level Agreements and availability

It is because of this increasingly high level of dependence on IT services that availability is so important. The management activities described in this module are required to underpin the availability aspect of Service Level Agreements (SLA), made between the IT service providers and customers, and/or to facilitate the implementation of Service Level Management (see figure 2). Further information on SLAs (including an example) is contained in the IT Infrastructure Library **Service Level Management** module.

2.2   Target readership

The target readership for this module comprises:

*   IT Services Managers, Capacity Managers, Availability Managers, Service Level Managers and staff, ie those responsible for ensuring that the customers' availability requirements are met

*   Computer Operations Manager, Network Manager and technical staff who require an understanding of availability issues

*   managers and staff who are actual or potential customers of a computer based service including services provided by a Facilities Management organization.

Although the guidance on contractual specifications applicable to the supply and maintenance of IT infrastructure systems is based on government contract documents, the guidance is easily tailored for use by non-government organizations since identical principles will apply.

2.3   Scope

This module is a guide to planning, implementing and managing IT services to meet customers' cost-justifiable requirements for availability.

It is concerned with the planning and operational activities required to manage the availability of IT services during normal operation and the application of preventive and corrective maintenance to meet availability requirements now and in the future. Guidance on coping with extended failures caused by major disasters is contained in the IT Infrastructure Library module on **Contingency Planning**.

The module is written from the perspective of the IT Services Manager, charged with the responsibility for creating an availability management function in the organization. Security issues as described in section 1.1 should be considered as an integral part of that function. availability management (and other infrastructure management disciplines) should of course be working to an organization-wide security policy, within which the security requirements of the infrastructure functions should be documented. Subsection 3.0.2, Security, covers in outline some of the organizational security issues which pertain to the availability management function.

Much of this module gives guidance on management activities that are required to ensure agreed minimum and expected availability levels are met, but it is also directed towards the planning, specification and procurement of new IT infrastructure systems to achieve required levels of availability of service.

Although guidance on how to design applications software is outside the scope of this module there are some suggestions for incorporating availability requirements in the software development process. The IT Infrastructure Library module **Software Lifecycle Support** will assist.

Availability management in the context of this module is mainly concerned with five topics:

* availability - the services being available to the customer when desired

* reliability - the ability of an IT service to perform a required function without failing, under stated conditions, for a stated period of time; the IT services' resilience to failure is considered under this topic

* serviceability - a contractual term which is used to define the minimum and expected availability of IT components as agreed with external organizations maintaining these components

* maintainability - the capability of an IT service to be restored to an operational state after a service break (actual fault-fixing is not the task of the availability manager)

* security - the module addresses the serviceability, reliability and maintainability functions of availability; the wider security implications are dealt with only in outline.

Availability is based on the whole of the IT infrastructure, not component parts: it is of course constrained by what can in fact be measured. Availability is a component of a Service Level Agreement (SLA) which covers the entire IT service, and is underpinned by a multitude of components, including hardware, software, networks and environmental equipment.

2.4   Related guidance

This module is one of a series that constitutes the CCTA **IT Infrastructure Library**. Although the module can be read in isolation, it is recommended that it is used in conjunction with other modules.

The following IT Infrastructure Library modules are related to availability management.

Service Level
Management

Deals with negotiating and managing Service Level Agreements, of which availability is one of the major components.

Customer Liaison

The module covering Customer Liaison may be of use since it explains the need for effective communication and co-operation between IT Services and their customers. This is important in servicing customers' availability requirements.

Capacity Management

Gives guidance on how to justify and establish a capacity management function, and the procedures necessary for the planning, implementation and running of that function. There is a need to exchange monitoring data and to coordinate plans and designs for new systems and services.

Contingency Planning

This module gives guidance on the measures needed to ensure continued availability (or at least to minimize interruption to services) in the case of a protracted loss of IT systems.

Problem Management

This module gives guidance on the control and prevention of problems which contribute to poor availability, and the identification of fragile IT infrastructure components. As such it is not only a major source of information regarding the reasons for unavailability, but also is the channel through which preventive and corrective action is applied.

Help Desk

Discusses, among other subjects, the handling of incidents (how to track and recover from service failures), which has the prime objective to restore normal service to customers after an incident as quickly as possible.

Computer Operations Management	Discusses many operational procedures relevant to availability, including backup and restore procedures, system startup and shutdown, monitoring of online systems, and the handling of failures.
Network Management	Gives guidance on the planning and control of common networks, and the management and operation of telecommunications equipment. The design of networks and the procedures to operate the network can be a major contributing factor to high availability IT services.
Change Management	Gives guidance on how to control changes to the IT infrastructure. A major source of reduced availability is ill-considered and uncontrolled change. Furthermore availability considerations should be part of the impact analysis process to which each Request For Change (RFC) is subjected.
Configuration Management	Identification and recording of system components is a key element in monitoring and reporting on availability. It is necessary therefore to define interfaces between availability management and the configuration management database (CMDB), which holds the IT infrastructure inventory.
Managing Supplier Relationships *previously called Vendor Management*	Explains how to manage relationships with suppliers efficiently and cost effectively. It is important that the Availability Manager and staff have a good working relationship with suppliers to ensure that products and services are supplied which meet the standards of quality required.
Third Party and Single Source Maintenance	Describes the use of independent organizations to maintain IT systems (mainly hardware). Serviceability requirements need to be agreed with suppliers. Compliance to the agreed serviceability criteria needs to be monitored.
Software Lifecycle Support	Discusses the selection of a lifecycle model for software development, ie from development to final decommissioning. Application software is a major component in any IT service, hence there is a need to consider availability and security requirements at every stage of development and live use.
Testing Software for Operational Use	Discusses the testing of software. Operational requirements for software availability is one of the items that needs to be tested.
Accommodation Specification	Describes the specification of IT accommodation, and also describes measures which can help to improve availability in the specification stage.

Secure Power Supplies	The use of secure power supplies reduces the number and duration of failures related to power failures, thus contributing to the high availability of IT services.
Specification and Management of a Cable Infrastructure	Discusses the specification and ongoing management of a cable infrastructure that can strongly influence availability.

2.5 Standards

The following standards are applicable in the area of availability management.

PRINCE

The planning and implementation of an availability management function should be executed as a formally defined and managed project. PRINCE is the recommended Government method for project management.

ISO 9000 series, EN29000 and BS5750 - Quality Management and Quality Assurance Standards

The IT Infrastructure Library modules are being designed to assist their adherents to obtain third-party quality certification to ISO 9001. Organizations' IT Directorates may wish to be so certified and CCTA will in future recommend that Facilities Management providers are also certified, by a third-party certification body, to ISO9000. Such third-parties should be accredited by the NACCB, The National Accreditation Council for Certification Bodies.

CRAMM

The CCTA Risk Analysis and Management Method.

Note : The standards detailed below are not referred to in this module, but some Government organizations and many private sector organizations make use of them:

Defence Standard 00-41: MOD practices and procedures for reliability and maintainability

These cover the following aspects of reliability:

* design philosophy

* apportionment, modelling and calculations

* prediction

* engineering

* testing and screening.

BS 5760 Reliability of constructed or manufactured products, systems, equipments and components

This standard covers:

* reliability

* reliability and maintainability programme management

* assessment of reliability

* reliability practices

* specification clauses relating to the achievement and development of reliability in new and existing items.

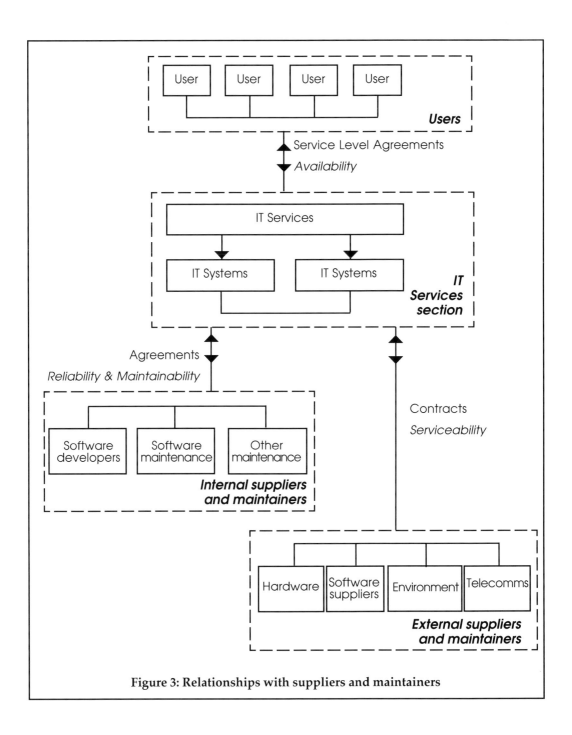

Figure 3: Relationships with suppliers and maintainers

3. Planning for availability management

3.0 Concepts

Availability management is optimization of the availability of IT infrastructures and the supporting organization providing IT services, to ensure that the requirements of the business (and therefore the IT Directorate's customers) are met. The availability of systems that provide IT services to the business is influenced, inter alia, by:

* the complexity of the IT systems

* the reliability of IT infrastructure components and the environment on which the systems rely

* levels of maintenance provided by suppliers or elements of self maintenance

* the IT Directorate that maintains and supports the IT services and the Infrastructure on which the IT services are built

* the procedures used by the IT service providers, eg Operations, Problem Management

* the configuration of the IT infrastructure used to provide the IT service.

In the simplest possible case the IT provider owns the systems which are provided and maintained by a third party. Appropriate conditions and controls can then be applied in the contract with that supplier about the availability requirements of the IT services.

As shown in figure 3, opposite, the situation is usually more complex. The IT infrastructure is supplied by several suppliers. The IT Services section provides support to the business. The configuration is often outside the control of a single responsible supplier. More elaborate management plans and controls are therefore required to meet the availability requirements of the business. This module is based on the situation illustrated in figure 3. Where organizations are based on the simple scenario described earlier it is a simple matter to interpret the necessary changes to the guidance provided in the module.

3.0.1 Terminology

The term 'availability management' is not unique to the provision of IT Services, practitioners can be found, amongst others, in industrial organizations producing complex products and services or with a complicated production process. This situation is one of the reasons for a profusion of incompatible terms and definitions.

For the purpose of the module and the benefit of the reader, the most important terms used throughout the module are explained below. More concise definitions of the terms are stated in Annex A.

Availability

Availability (or rather unavailability) is one of the key components of the quality of IT service perceived by a customer. Availability is underpinned by the reliability and maintainability of the IT infrastructure and the organization that supports and maintains the service. In summary, availability will depend upon:

* reliability of components

* resilience to failure

* quality of maintenance/support

* quality of operating procedures.

An IT service of the required availability, ie a service that a customer can use to fulfil required functions at the time that it is needed to fulfil them, is characterized by a low rate of failure and swift restoration of the service after an incident has occurred.

Reliability

Qualitatively, reliability of IT services can be stated as freedom from operational failure. The reliability of a discrete IT service is determined by:

* the reliability of each component part of the IT infrastructure used in providing the service, ie the probability that a component of the IT service will fail to provide its required functions

* the amount of resilience built into the IT service, ie the ability of the IT service to continue to provide an operational service when components of the IT infrastructure are inoperative

* the preventive maintenance which is applied to prevent failures from occurring.

Maintainability

In the context of this module, maintainability of an IT service is the ability of an IT service to be retained in, or restored to, an operational state. Maintenance, or restoration of the service after a failure, can be divided into five separate stages:

*   anticipating failures

*   detecting failures

*   diagnosing failures (finding the failed component of the IT service, including self diagnosis)

*   resolving failures (inter alia, taking actions to nullify the impact of a failure on the IT service)

*   recovering from failures.

Preventive and inspective maintenance to the IT infrastructure is applied to retain the IT services in an operational state.

Serviceability

The term serviceability is used to describe all relevant contractual conditions regarding reliability, maintainability and maintenance support for those components of the IT infrastructure for which an external supplier is contracted to assume responsibility. Where an external organization assumes complete responsibility for an entire IT service and its support (ie. when a Facilities Management arrangement is in place for an IT service), availability is equivalent to serviceability. This last sentence also applies to third party or single source maintenance.

3.0.2 Security

Security is often considered to be 'someone else's problem' and a 'technology problem'. In government it has been recognized that security is in fact a management issue and it is for everyone in an organization to be aware of all of the security issues of IT services.

The first link in the government security chain is the requirement to create and maintain an IS strategy, in which the IT Security Policy is considered as a strategic issue. Typically, the management and technical policies which are needed to ensure a justifiably secure IT service would be delineated in one document in the set of the organizational strategy documentation.

Detailed guidance about security is available to government customers in the IT Security Library. IS Guide C4 of the CCTA Information Systems guides can be referred to by all

15

organizations for a précis of the relevant information. The remainder of this subsection covers in outline some of the more important issues of security and risk management.

Security & availability

The needs of security are all pervasive, and this module recognizes that the availability management function is an essential component of overall IT security. Availability management is recognized as one third of the security 'CIA' tenet:

* **C**onfidentiality

* **I**ntegrity

* **A**vailability.

The overall aim of IT security is 'balanced security in depth': justifiable countermeasures being in place to ensure continued IT service within secure parameters (viz, confidentiality, integrity and availability). The Availability Manager may have a limited view of security, but that view must be in line with information supplied in the policy statement about IT Security Policy.

From the perspective of the Availability Manager, the following security considerations must, amongst others, be addressed:

* products and services must be available only to authorized personnel

* products and services must be recoverable within acceptable parameters, following failure, to ensure confidentiality and integrity are not compromised and availability is not further endangered

* products and services must be recoverable within secure parameters, ie without contravening IT Security Policy

* service contracts must be drawn up according to the security doctrine

* access for contractors to hardware or software should be restricted within clearly identifiable parameters

* data must be available only to authorized personnel at agreed times as specified in service level agreements

* countermeasures must be justifiable to meet the risks identified (see CRAMM, below).

From the above list it can be seen that availability management is a key rôle in the operation of an organizational IT Security Policy.

CRAMM

The CCTA Risk Analysis and Management Method (CRAMM), inter alia, describes a means of identifying justifiable countermeasures to protect the Confidentiality, Integrity and Availability of the IT systems.

One of the most basic of the principles is that every item of hardware or software and data must have a single identifiable owner. Availability and Configuration Managers need therefore to work closely to ensure proper identification of IT assets. Protective Operating Procedures (POPS) will be needed to cover the security needs of the individual infrastructure management functions. The IS Guide C4, Security and Privacy, provides more detailed guidance.

Risk Analysis and Management (RAM)

The general concepts of security **risk analysis** and management can be represented by a simple diagram with risk analysis and **risk management** being two related but separate activities, as shown in figure 4.

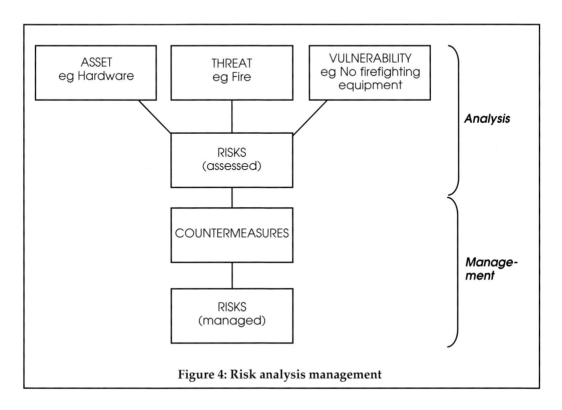

Figure 4: Risk analysis management

Risk analysis involves the identification and assessment of the level (measures) of risks calculated from the assessed values of assets and the assessed levels of threats to, and vulnerabilities of, those assets.

Risk management involves the identification, selection and adoption of countermeasures justified by the identified risks to assets, and the reduction of those risks to an acceptable level.

The concepts have long been held as valid and when applied via a formal method ensure that coverage is complete together with sufficient confidence that:

* all possible risks and necessary countermeasures have been identified

* all vulnerabilities have been identified and their levels accurately assessed

* all threats have been identified and their levels accurately assessed

* all results are consistent across the broad spectrum of systems reviewed

* all expenditure on selected countermeasures can be justified.

Formal risk analysis and management methods are now, more than ever, necessary to cope with the complex security problems presented by the rapid expansion of IT systems in support of business requirements.

3.0.3 Availability management process

To make sure that the availability requirements of IT services are met economically during their life-cycle certain procedures and systems are required. Plans must be made for two distinct responsibilities associated with availability management:

* **planning** responsibility to maintain availability in the face of changes to both the IT infrastructure and the requirements of the organization. Planning often results in the specification of new requirements and the proposal of changes (implementation of the requirements and proposed changes must of course be monitored to ensure that the achieved availability is as planned)

* **operational** responsibility including the collection of actual availability data, reporting on availability and the monitoring of compliance to agreed availability requirements.

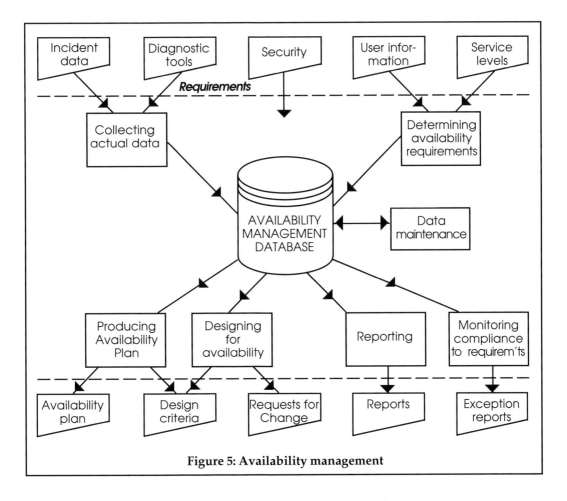

Figure 5: Availability management

Figure 5 illustrates the availability management processes. These activities and reports, and the systems required to perform them, can subsequently be the subject of more detailed plans to implement and improve them.

A short description of each activity is given below. Note that all activities are ongoing in a fully operational availability management function. The description in this section is only intended to serve as an overview on which a feasibility study for availability management (and any subsequent planning) can be based.

Planning responsibility for availability management

Activities needed to fulfil the planning responsibility are:

* **determination of availability requirements** - availability requirements for IT services are derived from the requirements of the business. Procedures and systems must be in place to ensure that all the relevant requirements of all the required IT services are identified and agreed with the business including availability.

* **designing for availability** - the primary task of the availability management function is to ensure that actual availability of IT services does not fall below the requirements. To this end, the availability management function is involved in the assessment of changes to the IT infrastructure, initiates changes to improve availability and participates in the design and development of new IT services by specifying the operational requirements regarding reliability, maintainability and serviceability.

* **designing for security** - see section 3.0.2.

* **producing availability plan** - to ensure that availability of all IT services meets the requirements, it is necessary to produce an availability plan periodically. The plan focuses on changes in requirements, IT architecture, technology and demand. Actions resulting from the plan must be monitored to make sure that the achieved availability matches the forecast availability.

Operational responsibility

Activities needed to fulfil the operational responsibility are:

* **collecting actual data** - in this activity the actual availability data of individual infrastructure components is collected and lodged in a database. This data provides the basic information for all other tasks.

* **data maintenance** - the availability management database is the central repository for the availability statistics which must be updated on a regular basis.

* **monitoring compliance to requirements** - this task is concerned with monitoring compliance of the IT Directorate to the availability requirements and the compliance of suppliers to serviceability requirements. Exception reports and plans for corrective action are generated when requirements are not met.

> * **reporting** - reports must be generated and presented to IT senior managers and to other IT Infrastructure managers, such as the Service Level Manager, who must be notified of the actual availability of each IT service.

3.0.4 Designing for availability

Figure 6 illustrates the contribution of availability management to the design process for new or modified IT services.

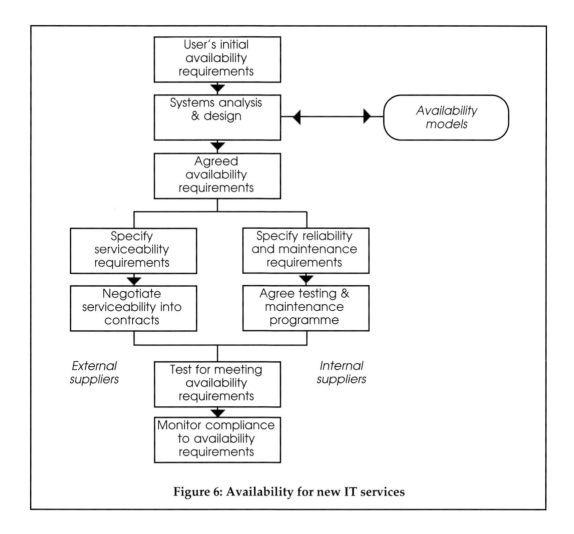

Figure 6: Availability for new IT services

Plan to meet availability requirements as follows:

*   obtain minimum availability requirements

*   analyze and design the service

*   test the design with a model of the service using estimates of reliability, maintainability and serviceability

*   redesign if the design does not meet all of the requirements

*   specify and agree reliability and maintainability requirements for components developed and maintained by the IT Directorate itself

*   specify minimum serviceability requirements for components procured from or maintained by external suppliers

*   specify procedures to test whether developed or procured components match the specified requirements (for example, software testing teams could be consulted about the availability requirements of new software).

To meet the availability requirements effectively and within cost constraints, a design should focus on:

*   improved maintainability of IT services (by planning to reduce the amount of downtime caused by incidents)

*   improved reliability of IT services (by planning to reduce the number of failures).

Liaison is required between the Availability Manager and the Problem Manager to ensure that fragile IT infrastructure components can be identified and where possible, made to be resilient.

Methods employed during planning can be divided into two complementary approaches:

*   the **statistical** approach which uses historical data and estimates of the reliability, maintainability and serviceability of individual IT infrastructure components to model and forecast the availability of overall IT services

*   the **deterministic** (or predictive) approach which uses information on the reasons for failure, to predict availability.

Guidance on some applicable methods and techniques can be found in annexes B and F. Note that deterministic methods are also employed in proactive problem management.

It may be of assistance to refer to the CCTA publication **SSADM and Capacity Planning** which describes the interfaces between capacity management and SSADM. Availability management will, of course, interface to SSADM at similar stages in the software development lifecycle.

3.1 Procedures

This section gives guidance on the planning required to implement an availability management function successfully. Although the following text is written with the assumption that an availability management function does not exist - in common with other IT Infrastructure Library modules - the guidance in section 3 is readily adaptable to any organizations, whatever the stage of maturity of their IT infrastructure management.

First of all, a project should be initiated and the Project Team members should be appointed. A prominent member of the team would be the Availability Manager.

It is recommended that the management of all of the work necessary for the design of the availability management function follows the CCTA PRINCE method. Use of PRINCE typically divides the work into two distinct stages:

* the feasibility study

* development and implementation.

Project Board

A Project Board should be created. This will provide overall guidance and advice to the Project Team and will monitor the Project's progress. Recommended Project Board members are:

* Executive - in some cases the IT Director, but if a senior business executive can be persuaded, then business interests can be seen to be represented

* Senior User - either a senior manager of the primary group of IT users or the Service Level Manager acting on behalf of the user community

* Senior Technical - the IT Services Manager.

The Project Board must appoint a project manager, who will manage all aspects of the work and will be responsible for deliverables and progress reports on the project. Other Project Team members are jointly appointed by the project manager and the Project Board. The most important appointment during this stage is that of the Availability Manager, who will play a leading rôle in the planning and implementation of the availability management function. The Availability Manager is a likely candidate for the position of project manager. See Annex C for a job description of the Availability Manager.

3.1.1 Feasibility study

A feasibility study should be undertaken to establish the importance to the business of the availability management function. The study must also elicit management commitment for the introduction or improvement of the availability management function by documenting the key management issues and benefits.

Typical terms of reference for such a study are:

Objectives

* to establish the need for availability management in the organization

* to quantify the costs, timescales and benefits of the implementation of an availability management function

* to identify the risks, constraints and possible problems facing the implementation of the availability management function

* to make recommendations for the successful implementation of the availability management function within the IT Services section.

Method

These objectives are met by:

* obtaining a clear understanding of the rôle of the IT Directorate and the needs of its customers regarding availability

* identifying the suppliers of the IT infrastructure and establishing the supplier related constraints regarding availability

* formulating metrics by which the effectiveness and efficiency of the availability management function can be evaluated

* establishing the effectiveness by assessing the current activities in the area of availability management and the effort that is put into these activities

* identifying any weakness in the organization of availability management activities and estimating the effort that will be required to resolve them (previous comments regarding CRAMM refer)

* identifying sources of information that will enable qualitative, as well as quantitative, analysis and planning of availability

* justifying the cost of introduction (or improvement) of the availability management function by implementation of thorough monitoring and planning techniques

* establishing the requirements for tools and evaluating any existing tools suitable for availability management

* examining the needs of IT security as outlined in the organizational IT Security Policy (with the help of the IT Security Officer)

* producing a detailed project plan for the improvement of availability management, showing objectives, tasks, deliverables, timescales, staffing, costs and quality control aspects.

Deliverables
There are two main deliverables from the feasibility study report:

* a preliminary report containing all findings and suggesting options for improvement, including a recommendation of the most appropriate actions

* a project plan containing details on the implementation of the availability management function, based on the favoured option.

The project manager will be required to present the study report formally, especially the project plan, to the Project Board. The feasibility study is now concluded and it is the responsibility of the Project Board to agree the objectives and scope of any further project.

3.1.2 Agree objectives and scope

The objectives and scope of the availability management function have to be agreed. Typical objectives include:

* to plan for, monitor and control the availability of IT services in order to match business requirements

* to improve the quality of the IT service by ensuring availability of IT services is at the minimum level required, within specified cost constraints

* to propose, introduce and oversee installation standards and procedures that will ensure that availability requirements are met

* to monitor relevant contractual conditions regarding the serviceability of supplied components and systems.

It is recommended that in consultation with others, and cognizant of the policies and codes of practice of the organization the Availability Manager actively contributes to the prevention of failures in all areas by:

* initiating and assessing changes to the IT infrastructure

* addressing the risk of changes to the IT infrastructure

* advising on the IT infrastructure architecture and the use of standards and procedures.

The scope of availability management is determined by the:

* scope of other IT infrastructure management functions, such as service level management, capacity management, problem management, contingency planning and change management; (see section 3.2 for a more detailed discussion)

* technology area; measures recommended by the Availability Manager may affect central hardware, networks, remote hardware, system software, applications software and environmental factors; it is recommended that the availability management function embraces all technology areas

* status of the function in the organization; measures recommended by the Availability Manager may affect the use of technology, the shape of the IT infrastructure architecture and the use of standards

and procedures. The Availability Manager must be given appropriate authority to introduce changes in all areas

* desired rôle of the availability management function, ie. advisory and active in each of the areas above.

Agreement on the objectives and scope of the function by IT Services management is essential to ensure management commitment to the project.

3.1.3 Mount an availability awareness exercise

It is, of course, necessary to obtain the commitment of the IT Directorate before the design and analysis of the availability management function starts. This commitment is also required to win the support of the personnel who interface with the availability management function. Commitment is best obtained by an awareness exercise. Circulars, discussion papers and seminars for interested parties can be used to gain support and to increase the awareness of availability as an important aspect of the quality of IT services.

The exercise should stress the benefits and costs of introducing or improving the availability management function. Use the example benefits described in section 6 of this module. They should also stress the possible problems resulting from the lack of a structured and effective availability management function, possibly using examples from the organization's experience.

Once implemented, availability management becomes an ongoing function like Cost Management, Capacity Management and Service Level Management. It is important to retain the commitment of IT Services management to the function, since the benefits of structured and effective availability management are not immediately visible.

3.1.4 Initiate systems analysis

The next phase of the project begins with the systems analysis required to design and develop the availability management function successfully. It is recommended that suitable methods and techniques from a method such as the CCTA SSADM (Structured Systems Analysis and Design Method) are used during systems analysis.

Sections 3.1.5 to 3.1.12 cover the main tasks to be undertaken, and design options to be considered, before actual implementation of the availability management function can proceed.

3.1.5 Analyze availability requirements

Identify - perhaps with the assistance of someone working within Customer Liaison - the business needs regarding availability of IT services. Whilst higher target levels are tenable there is no justification for committing availability of IT services above that which is required for the business. The requirements are best negotiated and stated in terms that the business customer understands and is able to deal with. The Service Level Manager should also be involved in the communication with the business customer.

Business requirements are not necessarily expressed in terms that the IT Services section is able to control directly. One of the functions of availability management is to translate customer and business requirements into quantifiable availability terms and requirements. Customer requirements are usually dictated by normal operating procedures and the nature of the business. Satisfying availability requirements will always however, be a compromise between quality and cost.

The business requirements for IT service availability should at least contain:

* a definition of IT service downtime, ie the conditions under which the business considers the IT service non-operational

* quantitative availability requirements, ie the extent to which the business will tolerate IT service downtime or even degraded service

* the cost the customer is prepared to pay for specified levels of availability

* service hours, ie when the IT service is to be provided

* any security requirement, as outlined in the Security Policies.

Note: once agreed with the business managers, compliance with availability requirements must be monitored. Procedures must be established regularly to review the requirements, since the requirements are likely to change through experience and changes in business needs.

Annex D provides more detailed guidance on the specification of IT service availability requirements.

3.1.6 Data collection detail level

To be able to influence the availability of IT services, it is necessary to influence the availability of individual components and to influence the availability of the IT service in total. The first step in influencing the availability of individual components is the collection of downtime data on individual components. This data can be used to:

* monitor IT service availability

* monitor supplier compliance to serviceability requirements

* assess the reliability and maintainability of components produced or maintained by the IT Directorate itself

* assess the effects of change on the IT infrastructure

* compare planned availability with actual results.

The Availability Manager must decide, in advance, the lowest level of components for which downtime data will be collected. It is recommended that the implementation of data collection mechanisms proceeds in a top-down fashion, ie from IT services at the top, down to all the individual components.

Choosing the right level in the component levels is a matter of achieving a balance between the value of detailed data and the resources and effort required to collect and maintain data. It is recommended that the lowest level corresponds with:

* distinct serviceability requirements, ie downtime data should be collected for each component that is treated as a distinct item in the contractual conditions with a supplier, eg if the contract specifies that repair or replacement of any broken workstation will take place in less than 4 hours, then downtime data should be collected for each individual workstation

* the Configuration Item (CI) level in the Configuration Management Database, ie the lowest level at which CIs are individually identified and controlled.

If there is conflict between these recommendations, the recommendation of distinct serviceability requirements takes precedence. For example if a terminal is broken down into separate CIs for keyboards and displays, but the serviceability requirements only specify the terminal, then actual availability data should be collected on the terminal, not on the keyboard and display unit separately.

3.1.7 Analyze sources of actual availability data

The organization should analyze the means already established in the organization to determine actual availability data for each component. This step can be accomplished by:

* identification of applicable data sources for each component

* determination of those configuration items lacking a data source

* an assessment of the degree to which each data source meets the data requirements.

At the data collection stage, data needs to be collected on each failure for each component. The following data items need to be collected:

* date and time at which the component became inoperative, ie the start of the failure

* date and time at which the component became operational, ie when the failure is resolved

* date and time at which the service was restored, when this differs from the date and time at which the component became operational.

The elapsed time between the first date and time stamp and the date and time at which the service was restored is the downtime for the service experienced by the customer. The duration of component failure is the downtime for the component and is related to the maintainability of the component. Additional appropriate date and time stamps may be collected to provide information on parameters that influence the downtime, eg the time needed for a specialist to resolve the failure.

For components serviced by external organizations data should be collected on the relevant serviceability requirements. It is recommended that at least the following data items are collected:

* date and time at which the external organization was notified of failure

* date and time at which the external organization released the component to the IT Services section in an operational condition.

Date and time stamps relating to other contractual conditions, such as the compliance with the contractual conditions, e.g. "a service engineer will arrive at the facility within two hours after notification", need to be collected too.

Useful sources of actual availability data are:

* diagnostic tools supplied by the manufacturer of the hardware

* information obtained directly from a manufacturer

* error logs and audit trails as produced by system and application software

* special purpose devices, eg power analyzers that record the number and duration of power faults

* the incident and problem management system: see the IT Infrastructure Library modules on **Help Desk** and **Problem Management** for further information.

To be able to use the data from these sources effectively, it is required that:

* failure information is related to the actual failing Configuration Item (CI)

* sufficient information is present to decide whether the CI is operational

* the data must have sufficient quality, ie be accurate, correct, and timely

* data items from all data sources can be converted into a common format and measurement quantity

* data sources supply data for most, if not all, incidents and failures that actually occur.

It may be that actual availability data cannot be collected cost effectively for every individual component of the IT infrastructure. If this is the case, less accurate but reliable options should be sought. To select options, consider the distinction between data required for:

* monitoring actual compliance to availability requirements, which requires detailed data on the actual downtime

* planning and modelling purposes, which requires less detailed data on the expected downtime, preferably based on statistical analysis of historical data.

For monitoring purposes, if no direct source of actual availability data is available, the options are:

* the use of downtime data from the incident and problem management system

* the use of average data if the data is present for all components of the same type, but not for individual components

* the use of a less detailed component breakdown (this method may cause some serviceability criteria to be lost to the IT Services section).

If none of these options is acceptable, explicitly exclude those components for which actual downtime cannot be determined from the specification of the availability requirements.

For planning purposes the same options apply to the collection of sufficient historical data to make realistic estimates of the anticipated downtime. In addition, estimates can be generated from:

* information on reliability presented by the suppliers

* the relevant contracts and operational requirements

* extrapolation of actual availability data from similar components.

The latter alternatives are especially applicable for new component types.

Recovery following
failure

It is important to recognize that a failure to deliver the IT
service may involve one or many of the following
components:

*   hardware

*   software

*   network

*   database.

If database recovery becomes necessary (and this is outside
of the scope of this module) the customer will perceive the
downtime to be the entire period between initial loss of
service and the point at which the service is once more
made available.

Recovery of the database may involve customers in re-
keying many transactions and it is important therefore to
recognize the impact of such difficulties. Availability
statistics will need to cover all aspects of downtime and be
capable of interpretation so that the actual cause of
downtime can be isolated. Section G9 of Annex G also
refers.

3.1.8 Availability management data storage

Procedures to store and maintain data must be established.
Such procedures are especially relevant to availability
management, due to the large retention period of the data
required. Procedures must be established for:

*   storing new data

*   condensing detailed data to information more
    relevant over the longer term

*   removing old, ie redundant, information

*   maintaining and reviewing data items held.

Data items that need to be stored include:

*   actual availability data for each component

*   IT service availability data

*   contractually agreed serviceability data

* data on the components used by an IT service, ie component identification and the relationships with other components (most probably available from the configuration manager)

* other relevant data, especially data related to the IT Directorate, the business of the organization and the IT environment that may correlate with trends in availability, such as shift changes, new software implementation, outside temperature and peak business activity.

The following options are available to store and maintain such data:

* the Capacity Management Database (CDB); the condensed data used in the CDB is conceptually similar to that required by the availability management function

* the Configuration Management Database (CMDB); especially applicable when the incident and problem control tools are linked to the CMDB

* the Capacity and Configuration Management Database combined; use the CMDB for detailed data and the CDB for condensed data

* a database specifically designed for availability management; when neither of the solutions above is feasible.

It is often practical to condense data after a predefined period. For instance, after using detailed data to report on the availability of a particular IT service at the end of a monitoring period, such detail is no longer required. Only the averages over the reporting period for that particular IT service need to be stored. By using consolidated data, storage can be optimized and maintained on-line for much longer periods. Ensure however, that where contracts specify, detailed historical data is available (though not necessarily on-line).

Care must be taken to ensure that relevant data is not discarded. The relevance of certain data items is not constant, but may evolve as the quality of the IT services provided improves, and different data items become relevant. Extra information might be useful after a major incident.

3.1.9 Plan monitoring of availability

Availability figures for particular IT services derived from Service Level Agreements should be monitored to determine whether the actual availability figures for the IT services match the agreed criteria. This can be accomplished in two ways:

*   computation of the availability figures from actual component downtime data and knowledge of the configuration, ie which components are used by which IT service

*   computation of the availability figures from incident data as reported by the customers.

It is recommended that both methods are employed, so that the results of one method can be compared against the other. If the results do not match, then either:

*   the computation of availability figures from component downtime data is wrong

*   the information concerning the configuration providing the service is insufficient

*   the reporting and classification of incidents is incorrect.

In all cases, plans must be made to analyze the cause of the mismatch and to rectify any shortcomings.

To be able to produce overall availability figures for IT services from component availability figures, procedures and systems must be established to:

*   determine actual availability data for all components used to deliver the service

*   validate component failure data

*   calculate the actual IT service availability figures from the availability figures for each component

*   ensure that information on the configuration (which may have changed over the monitoring period) corresponds with the data used in the calculations, ie is current.

For each **existing** service, plans should be made to investigate the configuration used by the service using suitable methods such as Component Failure Impact Analysis or Failure Tree Analysis (see Annex F). For **new** IT services the configuration should have been documented during the design of the service.

To be able to produce overall availability figures for IT services from incident data, procedures and systems must be established to:

* monitor and use only those incidents relevant to availability, eg an incident for an IT service handled outside the service hours in the SLA does not affect the IT service availability

* perform the calculations to derive actual IT service availability from incident data.

However, incidents out of service hours are also of interest to the Availability Manager. For example a failure (hardware or software) indicates a fault at any time of day or night: a night time failure may not compromise overall availability to the customer but statistics about the reliability of the failing component must be updated. It will be valuable to produce comparative data between the numbers of failures during and outside, service hours. In this way the true availability (and indeed the reliability) of components, can be identified.

3.1.10 Plan reporting

Building the reporting structure for the availability management function requires careful planning. Typically, reports cover the following topics:

* compliance with Service Level Agreements regarding availability

* the Availability Plan (see section 3.1.12)

* compliance of contractors to agreed terms (compliance to serviceability requirements).

Since reports can be requested on an ad-hoc basis, some flexibility in the reporting structure must be allowed. It is recommended that a short study into the required reporting structure is performed.

3.1.11 Verify ability to meet requirements

The availability management function must make every reasonable effort to ensure that both the actual and predicted availability of IT services does not fall below the agreed availability requirements. And when (as is inevitable) availability does not match these requirements, the Availability Manager must examine the reasons and discover whether or not action can be taken to eradicate similar problems in the future. This applies to both new and existing IT services. The Availability Manager plays an active rôle in:

* the design of the IT infrastructure and IT services

* the definition and implementation of installation standards and procedures

* the drafting and negotiation of contractual agreements with suppliers

* the promotion of good working practices.

Procedures should be in place that give the Availability Manager power to act when the availability requirements are not met. Furthermore, procedures must be established that incorporate the availability management function in the design of new IT services.

New IT services

For **new** IT services, the availability management function must translate the customer service requirements into specifications for the design and procurement of the IT infrastructure systems. The dichotomy between the cost of quality and the true needs of customers will be an issue whenever the availability of new IT services is being discussed.

For each component in the IT configuration the following should be documented:

* the required level of reliability

* the serviceability requirements (e.g. the operational requirement).

Procurers and suppliers will then have the information on which the maintenance programme of the service must be based. Care must be taken to ensure that the reliability and serviceability figures are expressed in a meaningful and verifiable manner.

The requirements for a new service with respect to the configuration of the infrastructure system components, ie the interconnection of the various new components to an existing IT configuration, and the organization of the support of the IT service must be documented too. For example, providing a Help Desk for customer support only during office hours for an IT service that is designed to be used 24 hours per day, 7 days a week will not satisfy the requirements.

Existing IT services

For **existing** IT services the same approach can be used to examine whether existing reliability, maintainability and serviceability levels correspond with the availability requirements. Both the requirements and the IT infrastructure that supports the IT service may have changed over time: availability modelling is required to ensure that the availability requirements continue to be met.

Modelling

The anticipated availability figures for an IT service for a specific system design or change should be calculated using appropriate modelling techniques. Various modelling techniques exist, such as:

*   analytical modelling, principally using the formulae in Annex B, is reasonably accurate, but tends to predict average availability, instead of the desired minimum availability

*   simulation modelling, which uses simulations of failures in a configuration, is more accurate than analytic modelling and allows finer detail to be investigated, but is also more time consuming and costly.

Results of modelling

The expected availability figures can be compared to the requirements. There are two possible outcomes:

*   the situation is acceptable, ie better than or equal to the Service Level Requirements, in which case only verification of the actual availability data against the predicted availability is needed. Contracts with suppliers will need to cover the appropriate conditions

*   the anticipated individual component downtimes are not acceptable. The provision of spare hardware items or alternative processing paths - built-in resilience - might solve the problem. If the predicted availability of the IT service remains unacceptable methods of improving the system design and structure must be adopted.

Improvements in the design should be cost justifiable. Some improvement, recommended because of security requirements, need not necessarily be cost justified if the improvement is essential to protect a valuable asset. The Availability Manager must prepare a case showing the cost and benefits of meeting the requirements.

3.1.12 The Availability Plan

It is recommended that the Availability Manager produces and publishes an annual Availability Plan. This plan, which is complementary to the Capacity Plan, should cover the changing requirements in availability of evolving IT services and include several scenarios to meet the IT services requirements. The Availability Plan should be reviewed and revised regularly.

To be able to produce the Availability Plan, the following procedures must be established on how to:

* collect the availability requirements from customers of the IT services

* reach agreement on the scenarios to meet changing requirements and changes in IT services on which the plan will be based

* determine the effects of the various scenarios on the service levels

* produce and publish the plan showing the effects of changes in requirements, where appropriate recommendations for meeting the requirements and the associated costs should be included

* obtain agreement on the results and implications of the plan with senior IT management and other IT infrastructure management functions, such as service level management (the Service Level Manager is responsible for agreeing any availability requests with customers), capacity management and cost management.

During the production of the Availability Plan, the Availability Manager must liaise with:

* the Service Level Manager, concerning changing customer and business requirements in existing services

* the Capacity Manager, concerning the scenarios for upgrading/downgrading of hardware, software and the network

* the Cost Manager, concerning the cost implications of the various scenarios for availability improvement

* those responsible for managing relationships and contracts with suppliers

* application development teams, concerning the requirements of new services

* software testing and maintenance functions, concerning the reliability and maintainability of existing services

* the IT Security Officer.

The availability plan should cover a period of one to two years, with more detailed information for the first six months. The plan should be reviewed regularly, with minor revisions every quarter and major revisions every half year. This schedule may be extended for IT infrastructures that are very stable, ie experience a low rate of change. It is recommended that the production and publication of the availability plan is aligned with the annual cost and capacity plans and the business budgeting cycle.

If a demand is foreseen for high availability services that cannot be met as a result of constraints in the existing IT infrastructure, budgets and plans, then reports need to be generated for consideration by both senior IT and business management.

Very high levels of availability can be provided to customers willing to pay the high cost of such availability. However the IT Directorate will inevitably have to make a case for any additional investment in the IT infrastructure and consider the charging policies needed to cover the cost of the expenditure.

3.1.13 Management reviews and audits

Plans must be made for regular reviews of the availability management function, and for audits to check that it is adhering to laid-down procedures. See 5.1.2 to 5.1.5 for more details.

3.2 Dependencies

Planning the implementation of the availability management function requires support from many groups and functions within the IT Services section. It is advisable that interfaces are developed with the following functions, which should, if not already in place, be planned.

Change management	An availability management function cannot succeed without proper change control procedures, in which availability management will play a rôle, through the assessment of changes to, and which impact on, availability aspects. Change control procedures are needed to keep the information for monitoring availability up to date.
Service level management	Part of the objective of the availability management function is to define the availability requirements for IT services demanded by the business. These are best obtained through service level management.
Customer liaison	The needs of business customers may be obtained from Customer Liaison personnel. It is probable that a customer liaison function will be the butt for complaints about poor availability.
Capacity management	Close liaison with the capacity management function is required to exchange data and ideas. Many changes affect both capacity and availability. Note that some improvements to availability may actually degrade performance at the expense of improved resilience/ reliability. In order to prevent conflicting solutions to the different planning options for change, it is important that plans are co-ordinated. Contingency plans will also be materially influenced by availability/capacity management.
Help Desk	The Help Desk is one of the primary sources of actual availability data for the availability management function. During planning for the implementation of the availability management function, the Help Desk might be the source of much information required for:

* sizing of the availability management function through, for example, the number of incidents or the incident information logged

* establishment of availability requirements, through assessment of customer complaints.

Computer operations/ network management	In many IT Directorates computer operations and network management functions traditionally have a responsibility for managing the availability of IT services. Quite often they also control the diagnostic tools collecting data on component reliability, maintainability and serviceability.
Problem management	An interface with the Problem Manager is needed since it will provide useful information on the:

* sizing of the availability management function

* means of monitoring availability data.

Assistance is also needed to determine the exact scope of the availability management function, since proactive problem management and availability management are closely related.

Software development

Liaison with software development groups is needed to obtain information on the customers' expected availability requirements for future IT services and also to participate in the design. Refer to the IT Infrastructure Library module **Software Lifecycle Support**.

Software maintenance and testing functions

Liaison with software maintainers and software testers is needed to obtain information on the reliability and maintainability of existing IT services.

Procurement

Liaison with those people responsible for the actual procurement of IT infrastructure components is required to establish procedures by which serviceability criteria can be negotiated and included into contracts.

Security

Liaison with the organization's IT Security Officer is needed (see also 3.0.2).

3.3 People

3.3.1 Availability Manager

The Availability Manager is required to ensure that the availability requirements are met and to advise senior IT management accordingly. He/she should have a good understanding of the challenges regarding availability in the areas of application development and maintenance, data communications, distributed IT architectures/ infrastructures, computer systems, computer security and environmental control, to improve the availability of IT services and to assess the effects of change on availability. He/she should also have the necessary skills to consider and propose changes in the organization and its procedures as a means of helping to ensure that availability requirements are met.

It is recommended that at least some of the following criteria are used in the job selection process:

* skills in statistics - skills in statistical analysis and interpretation of availability information

* communication skills - the ability to obtain and pass information to managers inside and outside the IT Services section,

* IT expertise - the ability to comprehend the design concepts of computer hardware, software, networks and their use and be conversant with environmental aspects

* comprehension of the business - the ability to understand the organization's business and to translate business requirements of availability management into IT requirements

* an understanding of the legal and contractual possibilities and limitations regarding serviceability requirements in suppliers' contracts.

In larger IT installations, ie those with more than 50 IT staff, or in IT installations with high availability requirements, the appointment of a full-time Availability Manager is normally justified. In other situations a part-time availability management function may be a viable alternative. Where appropriate it is recommended that part-time availability management is combined with part-time capacity management or service level management.

3.3.2 Availability management section

Sometimes the availability requirements and the size of the IT organization justifies more than one person in the availability management function. The natural division between actual availability data collection and reporting duties on one hand, and design and planning duties on the other hand, require different job profiles.

Collection of actual data and reporting activities are relatively routine tasks, that can be executed by staff with:

* experience in computer operations support

* systematic working practices

* analytical skills.

Designing and planning for availability requirements necessitates skills, such as:

* systems software or network programming

* a detailed knowledge of the IT infrastructure

* the ability to identify multiple logical solutions

* statistical ability and analytical

* interpersonal and communication.

During implementation of the availability management
function some other skills, such as programming, system
analysis and design, may be required, especially during the
implementation of the availability management collection
and reporting system. Staff with suitable skills may be
appointed temporarily to the Project Team as and when
required.

3.4 Timing

There are no explicit prerequisites or timing constraints that
impede the introduction of the availability management
function. For a fully functional, effective and efficient
availability management function, with scope and size
according to the requirements of the IT organization, it is
important that interfaces with other areas, as described in
section 3.2, are developed. Optimum timing criteria for the
development of the identified systems and interfaces must
be established.

The most notable interfaces are:

* incident control system; this must be well developed
before the overall availability figures of IT services
can be monitored; also to validate the predicted
effects of changes affecting availability: this links
closely with,

* problem and error control systems; these must be
well developed to ensure that the root causes of
incidents are investigated and recorded

* capacity management database (CDB) and
configuration management database (CMDB); these
must provide a reliable source of information.

It is preferable that change management is implemented
before availability requirements are set. At the very least,
some form of a formal change control procedure must exist.

During planning for the introduction of the availability
management function it must be borne in mind that the
production of the Availability Plan must be aligned with
the business budgeting cycle and the Capacity and Cost
Plans. The production of the first Availability Plan should
be scheduled to coincide with this planning cycle.

4. Implementation

This section describes the development, testing and implementation of the planned availability management function. It should be noted that the implementation of the function for new (greenfield) and existing IT infrastructures will differ. For instance, a greenfield situation enables design of an IT infrastructure where the production of availability data is an integral part of its day-to-day operations. The material in this section is of most relevance to greenfield sites. However, existing IT services will most certainly benefit from a review of current practices in the light of the material contained in this module.

4.1 Procedures and automated systems

In order to implement an availability management function successfully there are two main components that should be developed concurrently:

* procedures (since the majority of the work is to be performed regularly)

* support tools to support the function.

4.1.1 Procedures

Documentation

Depending on the level of detail of the information to be produced by the availability management function, daily, weekly, monthly and yearly operational procedures for all availability management aspects need to be set up and documented. In addition, customer manuals for reference, guidance and learning need to be developed. Because availability management functions will vary from one organization to another it is not possible to provide full guidance on which subjects to cover but it is imperative to document how and when:

* availability is monitored

* reports and plans are produced

* deviations are to be dealt with

* availability forecasting is carried out

* responsibilities are allocated

* security requirements have been breached and were handled (including reports, Protective Operating Procedures - see CRAMM in section 3.0.2).

Monitoring availability

Identify the timing of availability monitoring. Service Level Agreements should state what needs to be monitored regularly, and other aspects must be monitored on an exception basis. Ensure that the data collected is relevant to the availability requirements in the SLAs. In those organizations without an availability management function, it may be most effective to start with:

* IT services that are relatively easy and simple to monitor

* the IT service that is most critical to the customers

* the most critical components shared by several IT services, eg central hardware, systems software, network.

Reporting

The quality and effectiveness of the availability management function depends on the reports produced. The structure required to produce reports and the timing of reports should be carefully managed to satisfy the groups receiving the reports. Typically, reports include information to illustrate:

* non contractual causes of unavailability (application program or operator errors, environment, etc.)

* compliance with Service Level Agreements

* the Availability Plan (see section 3.1.12)

* compliance of suppliers to serviceability criteria, especially regarding contribution to downtime by maintenance suppliers (see also the IT Infrastructure Library module **Managing Supplier Relationships**).

It is recommended that regular reporting on service availability to customers is incorporated in the service level reports. Service Level Agreements should include availability criteria. An exception reporting procedure should be agreed with the customers. The purpose of an exception report is to inform customers of substantial deviations from the agreed requirements.

The Availability Plan must be revised every twelve months and consists of a detailed plan for the first 12 months, a global plan for the next year and longer term forecasts based on business forecasts.

Ad hoc reports will be produced as and when required. A clear procedure to determine both the validity of the report request and the requirements of the report should be established. It needs to establish:

* who requests the report

* who agrees that the report should be produced

* what the report should contain

* the recipients of the report

* how and when the report should be produced

* the justification for the report

* what resources are required to produce the report.

In general ad hoc reports are short and contain:

* a summary of the request

* the results of any analysis

* one or more proposed solutions to any problem investigated

* consequences of the solutions

* cost estimates for the solutions proposed.

Most ad hoc reports will be requested from within the IT Directorate and will tend to be technical in nature; in general they will not be sent to customers, but to the staff that originally requested the advice of the availability management function. Ad hoc reports intended for publication outside the IT Directorate must be prepared in such a way that the recipients will be able to understand the report.

Reports will help to improve commitment to the availability management function. It is advisable to limit the list of recipients in order to be able to:

* establish the need for detailed reports

* guarantee the quality of reports for the future before availability management is introduced.

Authors of reports should ensure that they are produced as specified and on time. Monitor if and how the reports are used to determine structure, the timing, the quality and the usefulness.

Forecasting availability | Procedures should be implemented to:

* assess the impact of changes on availability figures as a result of changes instigated by customers and other IT functions. A procedure that invokes availability planning in the impact analysis of changes instigated by others should be implemented as soon as possible after installation of the availability management function. In many organizations rudimentary availability considerations are already part of the impact assessment of changes

* initiate changes to improve overall service availability

* perform ad hoc studies on request. Possible subjects are:

   - implications of a new network topology

   - implications of an increase in the number of customers above the growth specified in the SLA

   - second opinion on availability projections by suppliers

* produce and publish the Availability Plan.

Deliverables from these procedures must be produced according to the specification. They have to be on time, and the level of usage by the recipients and effectiveness of the deliverables must be monitored.

Sufficient historical data regarding reliability, maintainability and serviceability must be maintained to assess whether designs will meet availability requirements.

4.1.2 Support tools

The systems needed by the availability management function consist mainly of three components that logically need to be implemented in the following order:

* availability management database

* diagnostic tools

* availability modelling tool.

Availability management database

The availability management database should be implemented as soon as possible after decisions on the data needed, the data collection procedures and the database structure have been made, since the data in the availability management database is a prerequisite to the monitoring of compliance to availability requirements by the IT Directorate and compliance to serviceability requirements by suppliers.

Diagnostic tools

The diagnostic tools chosen to support the availability management function need to be thoroughly tested before release for operational use. In most organizations it will be necessary to combine tools, some of which may already be in use to support other functions such as incident handling tools for the Help Desk. The following checklist can be used to choose and evaluate diagnostic tools:

* analyze tool requirements (see section 3.1.7), make a plan to evaluate against the requirements

* choose from

  - a combination of existing tools, in which case the additional effort needed to meet the requirements should be determined

  - procurement of diagnostic tools

  - development of bespoke diagnostic tools

  - a combination of the above

* procure, tailor or develop diagnostic tools

* install diagnostic tools if necessary

* verify that diagnostic tools meet the requirements.

Modelling tools and models

Whatever modelling technique is going to be used, one or more models must be designed and built. Tools are required (see section 7), which ideally should be able to interface with the diagnostic tools and the availability management database. To be able to use modelling techniques successfully in support of the availability management function, detailed availability data has to be at hand. See 'forecasting availability' in section 4.1.1 for additional guidance.

4.2 Dependencies

The dependencies are discussed throughout the module but success of the function greatly depends on cooperation between the different disciplines involved in the process of IT service provision. To achieve sufficient support it is necessary to supply information to all involved on the benefits of availability management in the delivery of IT services to the customers. See section 3.2 for more detailed guidance.

4.3 People

Personnel requirements are discussed in section 3.3 and throughout the module.

4.4 Timing

Estimates of the time needed to implement the availability management function depend on the number of procedures and systems that are needed for the availability management function and which ones are already in place. In a greenfield situation it will take from about 6 to 9 months to develop availability management depending on:

* the availability of support tools (which also depends on the hardware and software in use)

* the required level of detail in the collection of availability data

* how much activity is needed to monitor compliance to requirements

* expertise and experience of the staff involved.

5. Post-implementation and audit

This section covers the post-implementation review of the availability management project and the procedures for the ongoing operation of the availability management function. In addition, this section addresses:

* reviews for efficiency and effectiveness

* auditing for compliance to procedures

* reviews to ensure compliance with the IT Security Policy (to ensure that defined levels of security are both adequate and justifiable)

5.1 Procedures

A Project Evaluation Review (PER) will be necessary upon completion of the project to discuss whether timescales were met and budgets adhered to. The PER will precede a formal Post-implementation Report (PIR), which should be produced 3-6 months after the PER.

5.1.1 Post-implementation review

It is recommended that a formal post-implementation review, which could represent the final phase of the development project, is conducted three months after the full availability management function is put into operation. Reviewers should assess:

* whether the objectives of the project were achieved

* lessons from the project to be learnt for future projects.

Reviewers should check that the following indicators for an effective availability management function have been met:

* reports on deviations from contractually agreed terms regarding serviceability are correct and on time

* requests for change are promptly and correctly assessed for their impact on availability

* within reason, Service Level Agreements regarding availability are met effectively and efficiently

* forecasts on availability are correct and delivered promptly

* new systems and services are delivered with the predicted reliability and maintainability and comply with the availability requirements derived from agreed service levels

* requested reports about availability are accurate and on time

* interfaces to configuration management and the incident and problem control system are working and provide the necessary information regarding the configuration and its reliability, maintainability and serviceability

* interfaces to capacity, service level, and cost management concerning exchange of data and cross checking of plans are effective and efficient

* actual availability data is collected and recorded according to the procedures

* the Availability Plan is produced and published on time and provides sufficient information for planning purposes

* the IT Security Policy has been adhered to.

Note that the accuracy and timeliness of availability data, both recorded and forecast, may be influenced by factors outside the control of the availability management function, such as the projected reliability of new equipment provided by external suppliers. Steps should be taken to rectify any shortcomings, especially where forecasting availability and monitoring compliance to Service Level Agreements is concerned.

Other items to be included in the review are general indicators of the success of the project including:

* the number of IT service failures resulting in downtime - these should stabilize and subsequently decrease

* the quality (the intrinsic reliability and maintainability) of products and services supplied by external organizations - this can be assessed and negotiated objectively

* customer satisfaction, ie the extent to which disruption to business operations caused by IT service incidents is considered acceptable

* the satisfaction of senior managers (both inside and outside the IT Directorate) with the plans and reports produced.

The IT Services Manager is responsible for initiating the first post-implementation review. An independent reviewer must conduct the post implementation review.

5.1.2 Ongoing operation and review

The day-to-day operation of the availability management function covers many of the functions listed in section 5.1.1. Reviews on the ongoing operation should check that:

* activities required to manage the availability of IT services are being performed

* the availability management function produces results that are satisfactory to the business and operates within time and budget constraints.

A brief checklist of the activities is given below:

Daily/Weekly

* collection of actual availability data

* monitoring of compliance to serviceability requirements, suggest action when suppliers fail to comply.

Monthly

* produce and publish specified reports

* calculate and validate availability of IT services

* monitor and report on compliance to Service Level Agreements (SLAs), suggest improvements where SLAs are not met

* assess the effect of cumulative changes of supplied products and services on availability

* verify availability projections, investigate reasons for deviations.

Quarterly

* analyze trends in availability of the monitored components

* verify and adjust the availability plan

* review the performance of suppliers regarding serviceability

* review the availability management function for effectiveness, efficiency and the programme for compliance to time, budget and quality constraints

	* assess the accuracy of availability forecasts and data on which the forecasts are based.
Annually	* audit the availability management function for compliance to procedures under the responsibility of the organization's computer audit section
	* produce and publish an availability plan.

Ad hoc — The following activities are either initiated by the Availability Manager or on request from other IT infrastructure management functions and customers.

* impact assessment of changes to the IT infrastructure

* proposal of changes

* attendance at Change Advisory Boards (CAB)

* input to the design of new services or upgrade of existing services

* specification of Operational Requirements

* participation in contract negotiations

* input to SLA negotiations.

5.1.3 Producing the Availability Plan

The Availability Manager is responsible for the production of the availability plan. The following checklist can be used as a barometer of the suitability of the content of the plan:

* **review of IT service availability** over the previous twelve months. The review should cover actual IT service availability versus the forecasted availability and indicate major deviations from the forecast. The review should also consider the actual availability against the agreed availability requirements in the SLAs. The implications and causes of major deviations, in terms of cost and quality, to both the IT Directorate and the business must be discussed

* **details of scenarios** on which the plan is based. This section should reflect changing availability requirements for existing services and the implications of new services and major upgrades. The scenarios and their implications on availability should be discussed in business terms

* **all major assumptions** which have been employed during planning, eg "release of new versions of the operating software in the live environment may increase the number of failures causing downtime by 15 percent in the first two months after release"

* **discussion of solutions** that can be applied to help to ensure that availability requirements continue to be met (eg duplexing equipment that appears to be prone to failure)

* **all individual changes** to the IT infrastructure and its support that are required to achieve and maintain the required levels of service, and the dates when these changes will have to take effect need to be included

* **cost and capacity implications** of the proposed changes. Cost should contain both individual change costs, and the total cost of planning the proposed changes. This section requires collaboration with the Cost and Capacity Managers and cross checking with the Cost and Capacity Plans

* **forecasts of availability levels** for each IT service resulting from implementation of the proposed changes, including an overview of the cost implications throughout the year for each service

* **implications when recommendations are not followed**, expressed in terms of degraded availability levels and implications to the business.

The Availability Manager should check say, every three months whether operational activities and the availability of IT services proceed as planned, take action to overcome any shortcomings and, if necessary, make minor amendments to the plan. The plan should be verified at least every six months, amending the plan to provide more detail for the next period. A new availability plan should be produced and published annually. Activities to produce and publish a new availability plan may also be initiated by a management decision to change the IT infrastructure or to the organization that supports the IT services.

5.1.4 Review for efficiency and effectiveness

Many of the issues discussed in section 5.1.1 under the post-implementation review apply equally to regular efficiency and effectiveness reviews. Such a review is intended to show that the methods and techniques of the availability management function are required to produce the benefits of availability management. Periodic reviews can be held to ensure that:

*   the benefits of the availability management function are being delivered efficiently and effectively

*   shortcomings in the function are identified and corrected at the earliest possible date

*   the function is well managed by the Availability Manager

*   possible improvements of the availability management function are identified.

The main questions for an efficiency and effectiveness review of the availability management function are:

*   does senior management accept and implement the Availability Manager's recommendations? (investigate the effectiveness of communication, verify that IT Service Managers understand the rôle of availability management in the long-term provision of IT services)

*   is the availability of IT services satisfactory to the customers and does actual availability meet the agreed service levels? (examine the understanding of the configuration and incidents, the forecasting methods used, and how realistic are the customers' requirements regarding availability),

*   could the availability management function be improved? (investigate contribution of activities to objectives, effectiveness of procedures and support tools)

*   have the performance claims of suppliers and manufacturers been checked against contract conditions?

*   does the availability management function produce the right information, at the right time, in the right format, for the right people? (investigate satisfaction with provided reports and changes in the need for reports).

Reviews should be carried out by the Availability Manager at least every twelve months. It is recommended that the IT Services Manager annually initiates a formal review. The Availability Manager should produce plans, based on the information obtained during a review, to rectify any shortcomings. Reviews should be aligned with similar reviews in other IT infrastructure management functions, such as configuration management, problem management and service level management.

5.1.5 Auditing for compliance

The following checklist might be useful to those IT Directorates that wish to audit their availability management function for compliance to the procedures and advice in this module. It is recommended that an audit is completed at least annually. It is also recommended that the audits are performed by either the organization's computer audit section, which is independent of the IT Services section, or by an external organization.

An audit of the availability management function should check that:

* the communication of the availability management function with all relevant IT infrastructure management functions takes place and is effective

* reviews of the function are carried out regularly and as planned

* all Requests For Change affecting availability are assessed by the availability management function

* the potential benefits of activities that improve availability are quantified before work starts and afterwards that the actual benefits are recorded and verified against the plans

* compliance to serviceability requirements by suppliers is monitored and all deviations are reported and followed up until explanation is received, and if appropriate corrective action instigated

* all necessary reports are produced and published according to the agreed schedules

* procedures exist to collect, record statistics and maintain reliability, maintainability and serviceability data, and that these procedures are suitable for the purpose

* predictions regarding availability are made and validated afterwards

* suitable procedures exist to determine and calculate overall IT service availability

* determination of the availability requirements is an integral part of the application development life-cycle and is carried out at the appropriate stages of the life-cycle

* availability requirements are determined from and reflect service level requirements

* the Service Level Manager is provided with sufficient information on current availability and the possibilities for improving availability, to enable him/her to negotiate SLAs successfully

* availability levels and targets remain relevant to the requirements of the business

* the IT Security Policy is followed where appropriate

* all responsibilities and rôles are clearly defined and adhered to.

5.2   Dependencies

The dependencies listed in sections 3.2 and 4.2 are also applicable to the ongoing operations of the availability management function. The most important dependencies are:

* continued commitment to the availability management function

* desire continually to improve the service to the business (once more, cost must be measured against quality).

The major benefits from availability management, ie IT services will be there when they are needed, helping to ensure the realization of the business benefits the IT services were designed to provide, can only be derived in the longer term, as the collection of availability data and the quality of predictions upon which they are based improve. It will take one to two years before the availability management function, the IT Services section and the customers are sufficiently experienced in the rôle of the availability management function to realize the maximum benefits.

5.3 People

The IT Services Manager or IT Director should arrange for periodic audits of the availability management function by independent computer audit teams. Such audits should complement the audits and reviews which are regular features of a quality IT service.

In large IT installations the Availability Manager needs support to carry out the work. Routine tasks, such as the collection of actual availability data, maintaining the data, and production and publication of standardized reports, are best carried out by clerical staff. More complicated tasks, such as Request For Change impact assessment, ad-hoc studies and reports, availability planning and initiating change to improve availability, require different skills and are best performed by the Availability Manager or individuals with similar skills.

5.4 Timing

Timing of reviews, audits, reporting and operational activities is discussed in section 5.1.

6. Benefits, costs and possible problems

6.1 Benefits

The principal benefit of availability management is that IT services with an availability requirement are implemented, delivered and managed to meet that target. The IT services are delivered at a known and justified cost and to a predetermined level of quality and security which is concomitant with the cost and business requirements. Without availability management it is difficult to define service levels regarding availability that are measurable, comprehensible to the customers and relevant to the business. It then becomes difficult to decide what level of IT service availability is achievable and cost effective. Furthermore, without availability management, it is not easy to iron out availability problems and to gradually improve the availability of IT services. And it is difficult to hold contractors to contractual serviceability conditions. In summary, effective service level management is jeopardised by the lack of availability management.

Availability management helps IT service management to improve:

* **service quality** - because the service to customers is under control, availability management supports the smooth running of the business.

* **cost effectiveness** - by assisting the building of cost effective information systems that meet availability requirements, and by supporting the design and development of IT services including the IT infrastructure, which are oriented about the overall improvement of service availability. Furthermore a reduction in reactive problem support and a reduction in the amount of corrective maintenance and consequent reduction in the cost of downtimes will be shown. Availability management assists with the control of unnecessary expenditure on maintenance and resilience.

* **manageability** - by developing a full understanding of the strengths and weaknesses of the IT infrastructure. Availability management helps to improve supplier performance, and it delivers valuable and accurate input for service level negotiations.

     * **planning** - by complementing capacity management in planning, specifying and subsequently monitoring requirements for IT services and the IT infrastructure. Availability management promotes an effective and efficient use of staff and the existing IT infrastructure to meet the requirements of the business.

     * **security** - by ensuring that IT services are designed and recoverable within the secure parameters defined by the organization's security policy.

6.2　Costs

The costs of the availability management function can be placed under three headings:

Cost of implementing the availability management function

The implementation costs consist of those associated with:

     * personnel costs for project managers, team members and the members of the Project Board

     * development and/or procurement of tools

     * training of staff

     * awareness exercise.

Cost of ongoing availability management

The more complex and detailed the availability requirements are, then the more elaborate the availability management function will be. Consequently, the more elaborate the function the higher the costs for tools and personnel will become. It is, therefore, advisable to point out the likely high costs of ongoing monitoring and support activities for availability requirements for IT services with high availability requirements when negotiating service levels for new IT services. Costs are, of course, offset against the cost to the business of downtime.

Cost of improving availability of existing systems

Depending on the specific hardware and software in use, costs for improvement will vary. Redesign, re-engineering and retrofitting of IT services that do not meet availability requirements can be very expensive (in some cases even more expensive than building or procuring new systems). In general the higher the required availability levels are, the higher the cost of improvement and preventive maintenance will be. To be able to keep control over costs of improvement, projects should be carefully planned and the most critical availability elements should be considered first. Where high availability levels are already realized it will take considerable effort to improve the situation. Figure 7 illustrates the case. To go beyond the optimum availability generally requires considerable investment. A business case must be presented to justify such improvement.

**Figure 7:
Cost of improving
availability**

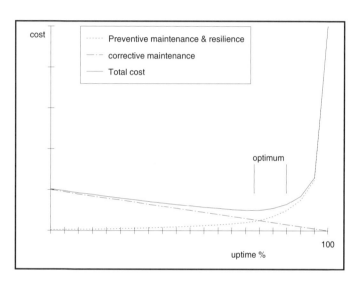

6.3 Possible problems

Availability management, as described in this module, is a fairly new subject to most IT Directorates and in many organizations staff lack the skills and experience needed to carry out the availability management function. Other problems that may occur areshown below.

Justification of costs

As described in section 6.2 the costs related to availability management can be high and senior IT management attention will be focused on justification. It is therefore imperative to include cost calculations, as well as the benefits to be derived from an availability management function, in every proposal for improvement.

Commitment

In availability management many disciplines come together that will not always share the same goals and priorities. In some instances a conflict of interest between responsibilities may occur. It is therefore important that the IT Services Manager is committed to the availability management function and promotes its importance.

Tools	In order to implement a successful availability management function, tools are required for different purposes. There is a general lack of tools specifically designed for availability management. Sometimes it will be necessary to develop bespoke tools. The development of tools can be very expensive and should only be attempted if it is cost justified. The cost of tools should be considered from the outset in planning the implementation of the availability management function. More detail on tools is contained in section 7.
Dependency on suppliers	In forecasting and modelling availability of new IT services it will be necessary to rely on reliability and maintainability data from suppliers. Sometimes suppliers will refuse to give explicit data on component reliability or to include serviceability metrics in the contract. For new contracts it is imperative to include serviceability requirements in the negotiation process. For existing contracts without serviceability requirements it might be possible either to renegotiate the contract, or, to terminate the contract and select a new supplier through open competition.
Determination of requirements	In determining availability requirements, customer needs should prevail. Where needs and wants differ, identification of the cost of different options will prove helpful. This will especially be the case for situations where customers are charged for IT services. It can be helpful to stress that the availability levels specified in Service Level Agreements are minimum levels of availability and that they might be bettered in practice.
Knowledge of IT infrastructure	Detailed knowledge of the IT infrastructure is a precondition for setting up the availability management function. If there is no Configuration Management Database it will be necessary to:

* take stock of all Configuration Items (CI)

* determine the relationships between CIs

* record all information about component availability.

The processing paths (the connections between CIs which are identified to facilitate the understanding of how a single failure can create a 'domino effect', causing further failures in the IT system) need to be determined. Registration of incidents and problems will have to be set up probably with the cooperation of the Help Desk and Problem Managers, to satisfy the need for availability information. It could then be some time before positive results of the availability management function can be shown and it may be difficult to retain management and customer interest.

7. Tools

An effective availability management function might require several tools. These tools are mostly shared with other functions within IT infrastructure management, such as capacity management, configuration management, the Help Desk and problem management. Tools described in this section are discussed from an availability management viewpoint. Guidance on the requirements of tools for other supporting functions can be found in the appropriate IT Infrastructure Library modules.

7.1 Types of tools

The following is a list of the tools which might be required:

* failure data recording and collecting tools

* database tools to store raw failure data and collated information relevant to availability management

* report generation and statistical analysis tools

* modelling tools.

Each type of tool is discussed in more detail in the following sections.

7.1.1 Failure data recording

Data recording tools are required to provide data on downtimes for IT services, and for individual components. Incident data at the customer level is usually recorded in the incident registration database used by the Help Desk and problem management sections within IT infrastructure management. Downtime data at the component level can be obtained from the incident/problem management system, if incidents are related to the failing Configuration Items (CIs).

Most of the downtime recording tools at the component level are aimed at specific parts of the configuration:

* central hardware (for example IBM SMF and RMF, VMS Error Log)

* network and remote hardware (for example IBM NETVIEW, SNMP agents)

* system and application software (for example IBM SMF, VMS Accounting, ICL TPMS, various DBMS software)

* application software (but is generally different for each piece of application software)

* environmental equipment (but is generally different for each type of environmental equipment).

The incident/problem management system is a useful source of failure data on passive components, ie components whose operational status is not recorded anywhere, such as cables and connectors.

To facilitate report generation and statistical analysis on reliability, maintainability and serviceability, it is advisable to convert the downtime data generated by the tools into a common format. The format should contain as a minimum the identification of the failing configuration item, and the various time-stamps that need to be recorded. See Annex H for details.

7.1.2 Databases

A database management system is required to hold and maintain selected and prepared data for reports, statistical analysis and availability forecasts. Databases can be either mainframe or PC-based dependent on the size and complexity of the infrastructure. See section 3.1.8 for more guidance.

The data that needs to be stored and maintained comprises three classes:

* unprocessed failure data provided by data recording tools; this is used to generate reports on the actual availability

* collated data from statistical analysis of the unprocessed failure data; this data is used as input to models in order to forecast availability and to review the impact of changes

* descriptive data on IT services, such as the relationships between IT service components and the IT services, serviceability requirements and technical specifications relevant to availability.

7.1.3 Report generation and statistical analysis

Reporting and analysis tools are concerned with the manipulation of data in the various databases. The tools can be either mainframe or PC based, dependent on the complexity of reporting and analysis requirements, the volume of data that needs to be processed and the location of the databases. There are general purpose tools like SAS and SPSS to fulfil this function. Interactive database query tools can be used, provided that they have sufficient functionality to perform basic mathematical and statistical operations.

7.1.4 Modelling tools

Modelling tools are required to forecast availability and to assess the impact of requests for change. Inputs to the modelling process are the collated and descriptive data from the database, projections of the availability requirements and requests for change.

A spreadsheet package to perform calculations is usually sufficient, when the modelling process has relatively simple requirements. If more accuracy or detail is required, availability modelling tools specially built for the purpose can be used. Unfortunately, there are as yet no readily available products in the marketplace for availability modelling of IT services. The use of modelling tools is therefore restricted to organizations that perceive there will be benefits and are willing to invest the time and money required to develop their own custom-made modelling tool.

7.1.5 Word processing and graphic presentation software

Word processing and graphic presentation software should be used by the availability management function to produce and publish reports, studies and plans.

7.2 Tool selection

All tools required for the availability management function should be procured using the following guidelines:

* define the formal requirements for the tool; describe and confirm functionality of the tool

* develop an evaluation method; determine relative weight of each requirement and produce a requirements matrix

* invite responses from suppliers; choose approximately three potential suppliers with known successful operational packages and reference sites

* evaluate bidders' proposals based on the evaluation method selected; contact reference sites, attend demonstrations and review bidders' documentation

* choose and implement a package; use PRINCE for the implementation project if the effort required for the implementation warrants its use.

More guidance can be found in the Information Systems Guides on **Procurement** (IS Guide B6) and **Evaluation** (IS Guide B7), and the Appraisal and Evaluation Library **IT Infrastructure Support Tools** volume.

7.3 Interface requirements

Tools used in the availability management function must be able to interface with:

* the incident/problem management system used by the Help Desk and problem management functions

* the Configuration Management and/or Capacity Management Database depending on the selected data architecture (see section 3.1.8)

* reporting, text-processing and graphic presentation standards used in the organization.

7.4 Current tools

Currently, there are few specialized tools for availability management available in the marketplace. The packages available concentrate on the reporting of actual availability of parts of the configuration and do not focus on the availability requirements of IT services. A number of individual data centres use bespoke applications to fulfil their requirements.

7.5 Advantages and pitfalls

The advantages of using availability management tools, like all tools, are that they:

* provide quicker results by saving time and effort

* are accurate in repetitive tasks and can handle large amounts of data, whereas people are better at deriving information from data.

The advantages are most apparent in the gathering and collation of actual availability data. This allows more effort to be directed at effective planning, the real benefit of availability management. The investment that goes into procurement and tailoring of tools has to be balanced against the objectives of the availability management function and the specific requirements of the business and the IT Services section.

There are many pitfalls. First of all, the tools are usually not readily suitable for availability management purposes and customization is often required. Secondly, the use of many different tools for failure data collection and the need to develop and maintain interfaces between all parts of the availability management function may direct attention at maintaining tools instead of managing availability. Thirdly, the skills required to make full use of the potential benefits of the tool may be hard to find in the organization, especially where tools need to be customized and, subsequently, maintained. Using a tool is very different to developing it!

8. Bibliography

IS Guide C7 Availability Planning: CCTA; 1989; (part of CCTA Information Systems Guides series); ISBN 0 471 92540 3;Wiley

System reliability modelling and evaluation: Singh, C., e.a.; 1977; Hutchinson

Reliability theory and practice: Bazovsky, I.; 1961; Prentice Hall

Engineering reliability: Dhillon, B.S., e.a.; 1981; Wiley

Reliability, management methods and mathematics: Lloyd, D.K., e.a.; 1961; Prentice Hall

Software reliability, principles and practice: Myers, J.; 1976; Wiley

Computer system reliability: Longbottom, R.; 1980; Wiley

BS 5760: Reliability of Constructed or Manufactured Products, Systems, Equipments and Components: British Standards Institute; 1986; British Standards Institute

Appraisal and Evaluation Library, IT Infrastructure Support Tools: CCTA, 1990; ISBN 0 11 330586 9; HMSO

SSADM and Capacity Management: CCTA, 1992; (Information Systems Engineering Library); ISBN 0 11 330577 X; HMSO

IT Security Library: CCTA, 1991; (classified "restricted", not available outside central government)

Annex A. Glossary of Terms

Acronyms and abbreviations used in this module

CFIA	Component Failure Impact Analysis
CDB	Capacity Management Database
CMDB	Configuration Management Database
CRAMM	CCTA Risk Analysis & Management Method
FTA	Fault Tree Analysis
IS	Information Systems
OR	Operational Requirement
PC	Personal Computer
PER	Project Evaluation Review
PIR	Post-implementation Review
POP	Protective Operating Procedures
PRINCE	PRojects IN Controlled Environments
RAM	Risk Analysis Management
SLA	Service Level Agreement
SLM	Service Level Management
SLR	Service Level Requirement
SSADM	Structured Systems Analysis and Design Method

Definitions

Agreed service time
: The times during which a particular IT service or system is agreed to be available, ideally as defined in the Service Level Agreement.

Availability
: In this module, availability is an umbrella term to also include serviceability, resilience, reliability and maintainability. A common definition of availability is shown below.

The ability of a component or IT service (under combined aspects of its reliability, maintainability and maintenance support) to perform its required function at a stated instant or over a stated period of time. It is usually expressed as the **availability ratio**, ie the proportion of time that the service is actually available for use by the customers within the agreed service time. This is calculated as follows:

$$\frac{\text{(Agreed service time - Downtime)}}{\text{Agreed service time}}$$

Downtime
: The total period that a service is not operational within an agreed service time (also applicable to IT systems and IT components).

Duplex
: Duplex equipment provides two, usually identical, IT components each of which is capable of performing the full task if the other fails.

Fault
: A condition that causes a functional unit to fail to perform the required function.

Failure
: The termination of the ability of a functional unit to perform its required function.

Incident
: An event which is not part of the normal operation of an IT service. It will have an impact on the service, although this may be slight and may even be transparent to customers.

IT service
: A set of related functions provided by IT systems in support of one or more business areas, which in turn may be made up of software, hardware and communications facilities, perceived by the customer as a coherent and self-contained entity. An IT service may range from access to a single application, such as a general ledger system, to a complex set of facilities including many applications, as well as office automation, that might be spread across a number of hardware and software platforms.

MTBF	Mean Time Between Failures
	The average elapsed time from the time an IT service or component is fully restored until the next occurrence of a failure in the same service or component. A shorter definition could be "expected lifetime".
MTBSI	Mean Time Between System Incidents
	The average elapsed time between the occurrence of one failure, and the next failure of a system.
MTTR	Mean Time To Repair
	The average elapsed time from the occurrence of an incident to resolution of the incident.
Maintainability	The ability of a component or an IT service, under stated conditions of use, to be retained in, or restored to, a state in which it can perform its required functions, when maintenance is performed under stated conditions and using prescribed procedures and resources.
Mirrored Disks/ Disk shadowing	Duplicated disks for concurrent updating - see also duplex.
Reliability	The ability of a component or IT service to perform a required function under stated conditions for a stated period of time. (See also, the mean time between failures - qv.)
Resilience	The capability of a set of configuration items (CIs) to continue to provide a required function when some CIs in the set have suffered a failure.
Serviceability	The contractual conditions with suppliers covering the availability of, and the conditions under which the contractual conditions are valid for, a CI or system.
Service Level Agreement	A written agreement or 'contract' between the customers and the IT provider which documents the agreed service levels for an IT service. Typically it will cover: service hours, service availability, customer support levels, throughputs and terminal response times, restrictions, functionality and the service levels to be provided in a contingency. It may also include security and accounting policy.
Service Level Requirements	A statement of service levels required by a customer (see also Service Level Agreement).

Annex B. Methods for calculating availability

B.1   Introduction

This annex describes some of the mathematics required for modelling availability and is intended for those readers who will be modelling availability, and those who will select and implement methods, techniques and tools suitable for modelling availability. The calculation of availability figures for systems, ie combinations of components or units, and IT services is primarily an exercise in the combination of probabilities and probability distributions. Turning these into expected (ie average) availability figures requires that the expected downtimes are assessed.

The statistical analysis of incident data and the forecasting of availability and reliability is a rich field of study in many areas outside the IT services industry, such as the chemical processing, electronics and aviation industries. The calculations and models presented in this section are fairly straightforward and provide adequate estimates. More elaborate calculation techniques are required when more accurate figures, or figures other than average or expected downtime and failure rate, are required. Such techniques can be found in literature on Reliability Engineering, which is readily adaptable to the delivery of IT services.

The models used in this section assume that:

* failures are independent, ie failures in one part of the system do not cause significant additional downtime in other parts of the system

* the failure rate for any individual part of the system is constant.

Although strictly speaking, neither of the assumptions above is necessarily valid, the results of using these approximations are reasonably accurate. For example, the expected repair time for a second failure close to the original failure, will probably be shorter than normal, as the service staff may still be on-site. Using the normal expected repair time for a second failure is quite reasonable when this type of repair does not occur often.

It is necessary to distinguish carefully between the average, or expected case, the worst possible case, and something in between. People are rarely interested in detailed calculations for the worst possible case, as this is usually no worse than the whole computer centre burning down, and thus being covered by the Contingency Plan. However, where a supplier guarantees repair or replacement within 8 hours, to assume that the average will not be better than this figure is to take a worst case assumption. Judgment and past experience are the only criteria which can be used, but consistency of assumption is important as is careful consideration as to what the resulting figures mean.

B.2 Formulae

Formula 1

$$A = \frac{(AST - DT)}{AST} = 1.0 - \frac{DT}{AST}$$

Where:

A = availability ratio
AST = agreed service time
DT = actual downtime during agreed service time

See Annex A for the definition of terms. As a percentage the availability ratio is 100 times the figure obtained by using formula (1). Formula (1) is suitable for calculating the availability ratio of new services and is also applicable when calculating the availability ratio of a service that exists, ie assuming that the downtimes of the IT service have been recorded. However, given the expected downtimes or availability ratios of individual units it is not always suitable for predicting, ie modelling, the availability ratio of the total infrastructure. The method of calculation for series and parallel chains provides a more accurate picture.

Formula 2

For N units in series with availability ratios of A_1, A_2, ... A_N, the availability ratio of the total system A_{Total} is given by the product of individual ratios, thus:

$$A_{Total} = A_1 \times A_2 \times ..... A_N$$

Formula 3

For the availability ratio of M units or more, working out of N like units with availability ratio A in parallel, the binomial distribution is appropriate and is given by:

$$A_{Total} = \sum_{M=1}^{N} \frac{N! \ A^M \ (1-A)^{N-M}}{M! \ (N-M)!}$$

where N! is the product of all the integers between 1 and N, eg. 3! is 6 (3 x 2 x 1).

Formula 4

Quite frequently, it is necessary to predict the availability ratio of a subsystem, which has 2 units in parallel, such that a satisfactory service is delivered if either one or both units are working. In this case, using formula (3) with $N = 2$, and $M = 1$ and 2, and taking the sum, gives:

$$A_{Total} = 2A - A^2$$

There is a very low probability that the second of the parallel units will fail in the downtime appropriate to the first of the units.

B.3 Example 1 - A simple infrastructure

The configuration consists of the central processing unit and 2 disk drives as shown in figure B1. The data used in the subsequent availability ratio calculations for example 1 are given in figure B2. In this and the following examples the failures are quoted on a per year basis, for the sake of convenience. It is more usual to see them quoted per 10,000 hours, which is unambiguous.

**Figure B1:
Example 1 -
configuration**

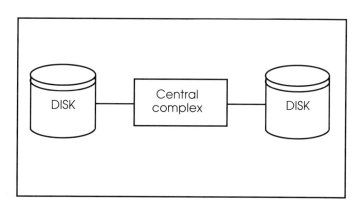

**Figure B2:
Failure rates
by subsystem**

Subsystem	Failures Per Year	Repair Time Per Failure (Hours)	Recovery Time Per Failure (Hours)
Central Complex	4	4	1
Disk Drive	2	2	3

Service hours: 8 hours a day and 5 days a week

$$= 8 \times 5 \times 52$$
$$= 2080 \text{ hours a year}$$

In practical situations, the figure for the expected failure rate can be based on information from the suppliers, past experience and historical data. The figures for the expected repair and recovery time per failure can be based on past experience, historical data and the serviceability criteria in the maintenance contract. Note that the serviceability criteria alone are not sufficient, because estimates of the time the IT Services section needs to find the fault and to restore the service after the fault has been repaired must be taken into account as well.

B.3.1 Case 1

The service can only continue if both drives are working. Therefore, the infrastructure can be assumed to have the characteristics shown in figure B3, ie 3 units in series.

Figure B3:
Example 1 -
case 1, series chain

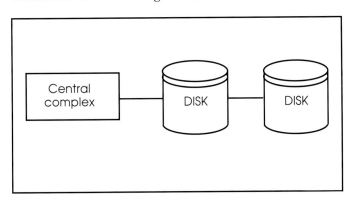

Formula 5

Using the data from figure B2, the following can be written:

$$CCDT = CCNF * (CCRT + CCST)$$
$$= 4 * (4 + 1)$$
$$= 20 \text{ Hours}$$

$$SDDT = SDNF * (SDRT + SDST)$$
$$= 2 * (2 + 3)$$
$$= 10 \text{ Hours}$$

Where:

CCDT =	Central complex downtime
CCNF =	Number of central complex failures
CCRT =	Central complex repair time
CCST =	Central complex recovery time
SDDT =	Single Disk drive downtime
SDNF =	Single Disk drive number of failures
SDRT =	Single Disk drive repair time
SDST =	Single Disk drive recovery time.

Formula 6

The availability ratios, calculated with formula (1) are:

$$A_C = \frac{(AST - CCDT)}{AST} = \frac{(2080 - 20)}{2080}$$

$$= 0.9903846 \text{ or } 99.04 \text{ percent}$$

$$A_D = \frac{(AST - SDDT)}{AST} = \frac{(2080 - 10)}{2080}$$

$$= 0.9951923 \text{ or } 99.52 \text{ percent}$$

Where:

A_C = Central complex availability ratio
A_D = Single Disk drive availability ratio
AST = Agreed service time

Formula 7

The availability ratio for the service provided by the infrastructure is from (2) given by the product of the availability ratios for the central complex and 2 disk drives, ie:

$$A_{Total} = A_C * A_D^2$$

$$= 0.9903846 * 0.9951923^2$$

$$= 0.9808845 \text{ or } 98.09 \text{ percent}$$

This last figure implies an average downtime of 3.3 hours a month.

B.3.2 Case 2

The service can continue if either disk drive fails. The availability ratios of the subsystems are the same as in case 1. This time, for calculating the availability ratio, consider the central complex to be in series with the two disk drives, which are in parallel, as shown in figure B4.

Figure B4:
Example 1 -
case 2, disks
in parallel

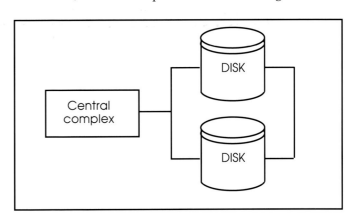

Formula 8

From (4) the availability ratio is given by:

$$A_{DD} = 2 * A_D - A^2_D$$

$$= 2 * 0.9951923 - 0.9951923^2$$

$$= 0.9999769 \text{ or almost } 100 \text{ percent}$$

Where:

$$A_{DD} = \text{Double disk drive availability ratio}$$

Formula 9

The system can now be considered to consist of a series chain, and hence from (2), the availability ratio is given by:

$$A_{Total} = A_C * A_{DD}$$

$$= 0.9903846 * 0.9999769$$

$$= 0.9903617 \text{ or } 99.04 \text{ percent}$$

or an availability ratio of 99 percent. This last figure implies an average downtime of 1.65 hours every month.

Compared with case 1, the downtime has approximately been halved by using the disks in parallel and is nearly equal to the downtime of the central complex alone, which is not surprising since the parallel operation of the disks almost completely eliminates downtime due to disk failure.

B.3.3 Case 3

The service can run if either disk drive fails but the service must be stopped, and then recovered. Hence, the infrastructure can be considered to be a hybrid of cases 1 and 2, in that the disk repair is in parallel and the disk recovery is in series. The series and parallel chains are shown in figure B5.

**Figure B5:
Example 1 -
case 3, parallel
disk repair, serial
disk recovery**

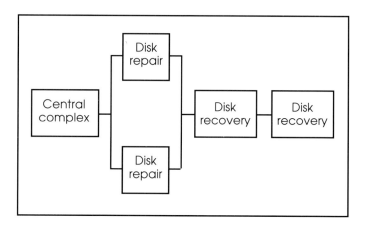

Once again (1) is used to calculate the availability ratios, which along with the downtimes due to repair and recovery, taken from figure B2 are given in figure B6.

From (4), the availability ratio of the two disk drives for the repair in parallel, is given by

$$2 * 0.9961538 - 0.9961538^2 = 0.9999853$$

The availability ratio for the service provided by the system is now a simple in series calculation, ie using this last result and the availability ratios for the other subsystem from figure B6 in (2) to obtain

$$0.9903846 * 0.9999853 * 0.9990385^2 = 0.9884664$$

or an availability ratio of 98.8 percent. This last figure implies an average downtime of 4.0 hours every 2 months, a slightly worse result to that in case 2.

Figure B6:
Downtimes
by subsystem

Subsystem	Downtime Per Year (Hours)	Availability Ratio
Central Complex	20	0.9903846
Disk Drive (repair)	8	0.9961538
Disk Drive (recovery)	2	0.9990385

B.4 Example 2 - A larger infrastructure

The configuration is shown in figure B7. It is assumed the service is required during 2920 hours a year. All 8 terminals are required at site A, but only 6 out of 9 at site B for the service to be acceptable. It is required to calculate the average availability ratio at each site. The data used in the subsequent availability ratio calculations are given in figure B8.

Use (1) to calculate the availability ratios, which along with the downtimes per sub-system, are given in figure B9.

**Figure B7:
Example 2,
configuration**

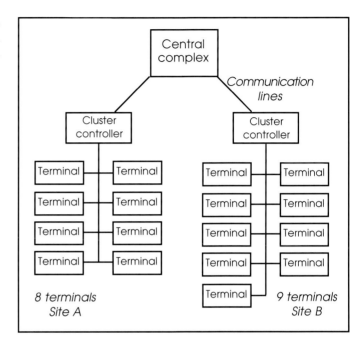

**Figure B8:
Failure rates
by subsystem**

Subsystem	Failures per year	Repair time per failure (Hours)	Recovery time per failure (Hours)
Central Complex	8	6	0.5
Comms line	4	8	0
Cluster controller	1	8	0
Terminal & cable	1	8	0

**Figure B9:
Downtimes
by subsystem**

Subsystem	Downtime per year (Hours)	Availability Ratio
Central Complex	52	0.9821918
Comms line	32	0.9890411
Cluster controller	8	0.9972603
Terminal & cable	8	0.9972603
Service required for 2920 hours per year		

Figure B10:
Example 2,
Site A

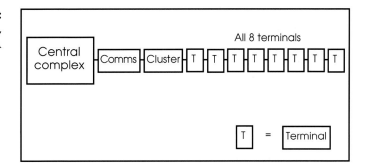

Formula 10

The service is not considered to be satisfactory unless all 8 terminals are working. Hence, the availability ratio for the service provided by the system is given by the product of the availability ratios as in example 1 case 1, ie from (2):

$$A_{Total} = CCA * CLA * CUA * TMA^8$$

$$= 0.9477361$$

which after multiplying by 100 and working to 3 significant figures gives an availability ratio of 94.8 percent. This last figure implies an average downtime of 12.7 hours a month.

Figure B11:
Example 2
- site B

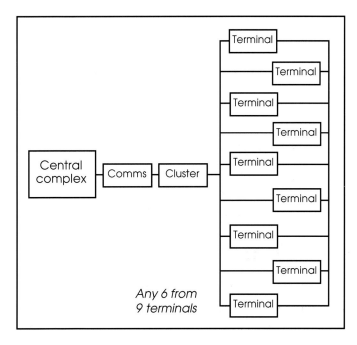

Formula 11

The service is considered satisfactory when 6 or more of the 9 terminals are working.

Formula (3) is appropriate to calculate the availability ratio for the terminals. Therefore, the probability of 6 or more, of the 9 working is equal to the sum of the probabilities of 6, 7, 8 and 9 terminals working, which is given by:

$$TCA = \frac{9! * TMA^6 * (1 - TMA)^3}{3! * 6!} +$$

$$\frac{9! * TMA^7 * (1 - TMA)^2}{2! * 7!} +$$

$$\frac{9! * TMA^8 * (1 - TMA)}{1! * 8!} +$$

$$\frac{9! * TMA^9}{0! * 9!}$$

$$= \quad 1 \text{ (to 7 decimal places)}$$

The availability ratio calculation is now a series chain calculation, ie from (2) 0.9687666 or an availability ratio of 96.9 percent. This last figure implies an average downtime of 7.6 hours a month.

B.5   Conclusion

The formulae and examples in this section are relatively simple. Mathematical theory is generally available in the literature to deal with more complex problems, such as:

* treatment of parallel chains with unequal availabilities in the components

* more accurate calculations of the failure rate in IT infrastructures

* treatment of correlation between failures in separate components.

For most IT infrastructures the calculations can become quite involved. It is recommended that suitable tools are employed to model availability.

Annex C. Example job description - Availability Manager

Main duties

1   Specifies and maintains all procedures required for the availability management function.

2   Supervises the collection of reliability, maintainability and serviceability data on all configuration items (from monitors and from company statistics).

3   Assesses the impact of Requests For Change on availability and attends Change Advisory Board (CAB) meetings, when appropriate.

4   Responsible for ensuring that the availability criteria of Service Level Agreements are met.

5   Publicizes the availability management function to the organization, ensures that all relevant staff are familiar with procedures.

6   Analyzes and reviews the availability management function on a regular basis to ensure its effectiveness and efficiency, plans for audits, recommends improvements where needed.

7   Produces and publishes the Availability Plan discussing the ability of the IT infrastructure to meet the availability requirements of the business.

8   Responsible for initiating changes to ensure that availability requirements are met and to improve availability beyond the required level within cost constraints.

9   Responsible for monitoring compliance of IT suppliers, as well as the IT Directorate itself, to contractual conditions regarding serviceability. Participates in the negotiation and management of contracts with suppliers to underpin the Service Level Agreements.

10 Advises the IT Directorate, the Service Level Manager and Application Development Teams on issues regarding availability.

11 Ensures that availability requirements of new IT services can be met by determining the reliability, maintainability and serviceability requirements from the design.

12   Advises on the availability requirements of new services in relation to obtaining the proper cost/quality balance.

13   Maintains an awareness of advances in availability management eg new tools produced.

Annex D. Determining availability requirements

This annex discusses the various technical issues involved in determining the availability requirements of IT services. The specification of availability requirements includes:

*   definition of IT service downtime, ie the conditions under which the customer considers the IT service not to be operational

*   service hours

*   availability metrics.

Note that it is not easy to specify the requirements, since customers generally do not consider availability as the prime metric for judging the quality of the IT service.

Determining the requirements is an iterative process, where business requirements ultimately need to balance against the cost. The necessary steps are:

*   determine business availability requirements

*   from the business requirements specify reliability and maintainability requirements for those parts of the IT service under responsibility of the IT Directorate, and serviceability requirements for each supplier

*   estimate the cost of meeting reliability, maintainability and serviceability requirements

*   determine whether the cost of meeting business availability requirements is justified

*   if cost justified, make agreements within the IT Directorate on reliability and maintainability criteria, negotiate serviceability criteria into contracts with suppliers

*   if costs are not justified, enter re-negotiations with customers.

Note that business requirements may change over time. Essentially the same steps will have to be taken to ensure that the availability requirements of the business continue to be met.

D.1 Defining downtime

Before actual availability levels are negotiated, a suitable definition of downtime for an IT service must be obtained. The aim is to agree on a definition of an operational service that is clear to both customer and IT Directorate. The definition of downtime is usually determined by the nature of the service and the requirements of the business.

Although most failures will tend to cause loss of the entire service, some will cause loss of only part of the service or will prevent the customer from making use of a required function. Some failures will not affect any customer. A definition of downtime is required to avoid disputes over service availability. The definition involves:

* the **required functions** of the IT service, which can be sometimes derived from the design documentation

* the **delivery point** of the required functions, eg failure of a terminal owned and maintained by the business, may not contribute to downtime

* the **conditions** under which the required functions are supplied, eg failure of an online transaction due to input mistakes by customers does not contribute to downtime.

An IT service is unavailable if any of the required functions at any delivery point cannot be used, while the conditions under which the IT service is supplied are met.

In addition, the following issues need to be resolved:

* **different requirements over time** - different levels of availability may be permitted over differing time periods

* **configuration** - some parts of the configuration do not need to be operational for the service to be available.

D.2 Specifying service hours

The next step in specifying the availability requirements is the specification of the required service hours. When specifying the service hours, the following points should be taken into account:

* the agreed service time for regular use, eg "the service is available from 8 am to 6 pm on each working day"

* procedures for scheduling service hour extensions, eg for the benefit of customers working late, and to calculate the cost involved

* scheduled maintenance during service hours, eg time needed by the IT Services section for scheduled maintenance, applies especially to IT Directorates that need to deliver a service 24 hours a day.

Incidents reported by customers outside regular service hours and scheduled service hour extensions may not contribute to the availability figures in Service Level Agreements.

D.3 Availability metrics

The final part of specifying availability requirements is the specification of the availability metrics for the IT service.

Metrics can be categorized as follows:

* the duration of periods of downtime, eg availability ratio, mean time to repair

* the frequency of periods of downtime, eg failure rate, mean time between failures (reliability)

* fluctuations in the above, eg standard deviation of failure rate, time to repair.

The following considerations must be taken into account when specifying availability metrics.

* **presentation** - the format in which the metrics are presented to the customer, eg 97.5 percent availability ratio or 4 hours total downtime in a period of four weeks, of 8 hour working days

* **kind of metric** - the following metrics can be applied

    - average

    - minimum (or maximum)

    - percentiles.

* **sampling period and method** - aggregation levels, methods and periods should be carefully planned. The following methods are applicable:

    - report over a fixed period, eg availability ratio in a certain week, month, quarter or year. A short period usually shows a great variance in the values produced.

    - report over a rolling period, eg the availability ratio as a moving average over the last quarter. Rolling periods tend to show trends, but obscure fluctuations.

It is recommended that availability metrics for IT services are specified as:

* minimum availability ratio as percentage over a period of one month

* maximum number of failures per month

* maximum downtime per incident

* average availability ratio as a moving average over the last quarter.

These recommendations may need to be adapted to suit the requirements of the business.

Annex E. Availability and incidents

All metrics are derived from the various stages that follow an incident. Figure E1 gives an overview of these stages and some of the metrics.

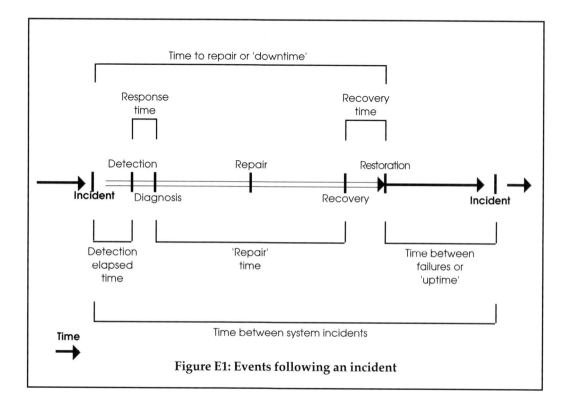

Figure E1: Events following an incident

Every incident passes through several major stages. The time elapsed in these stages may vary considerably. The following example, a blank terminal screen, illustrates these stages. Although the example covers a hardware failure, similar considerations apply to all configuration items used to provide the service.

* **Incident start** - the customer is aware of a blank screen.

* **Incident detection** - the Help Desk is notified of the incident by the customer.

* **Incident diagnosis** - the Help Desk instigates action to determine the cause of the incident, in this case a failure in a cluster controller.

* **Incident repair** - after being notified by the Help Desk, the supplier repairs the cluster controller. It is useful to split the time into

  - time taken to attend

  - time taken to repair

* **Incident restoration/recovery** - after the supplier has notified the Help Desk, that the cluster controller has been repaired, terminal lines need to be reset to make the service available to the customer, ie to fully restore the service. Note that recovery of the service, and recovery to the point at which the service can be restored to the customer are often two discrete operations.

Each stage in the example above influences the total downtime as perceived by the customer. To the customer the mean time to repair (MTTR) is determined by the onset and satisfactory resolution of the incident. The supplier on the other hand uses a totally different concept of mean time to repair in serviceability specifications. To the supplier the mean time to repair is determined only by the time the supplier is notified of the fault and the time at which the supplier notifies the IT Services section of successful repair. Statistics must reflect this disparity and customers must be made aware of the distinctions.

To the IT Services section the other stages are important as well. Reducing the time spent in the various stages offers considerable opportunities to improve availability.

Annex F. Techniques for analyzing availability

This annex introduces two techniques commonly used to analyze availability. They are:

* Component Failure Impact Analysis or CFIA

* Fault Tree Analysis or FTA.

In conjunction with the calculation methods discussed in Annex B, these techniques provide an analytic framework for forecasting availability.

F.1 Component Failure Impact Analysis

Component Failure Impact Analysis is a relatively simple technique introduced by IBM. Its main benefits are:

* quick location of vulnerable configuration items and services

* ease of use.

The first step in CFIA is to draw a grid with configuration items on one axis and receivers of the IT service on the other axis. The next step is to perform the following procedure at each intersection point in the grid:

* leave a blank when a failure of the configuration item does not affect the IT service in any way.

* insert an 'X' when a failure of the configuration item causes the IT service to be inoperative.

* insert an 'A' when there is an alternative configuration item to provide the service.

* insert a 'B' when there is an alternative configuration item, but the service has to be recovered first.

Figure F1 contains a completed grid for the configuration shown(overleaf).

The last step is to analyze the grid. Configuration items that have a large number of Xs mean that a large number of services are affected by a failure in those configuration items. IT services with a large number of Xs are complex and are vulnerable to failures.

Refinements of this technique, including more detailed data on the availability of components, will improve the findings, but will also increase the difficulty of use.

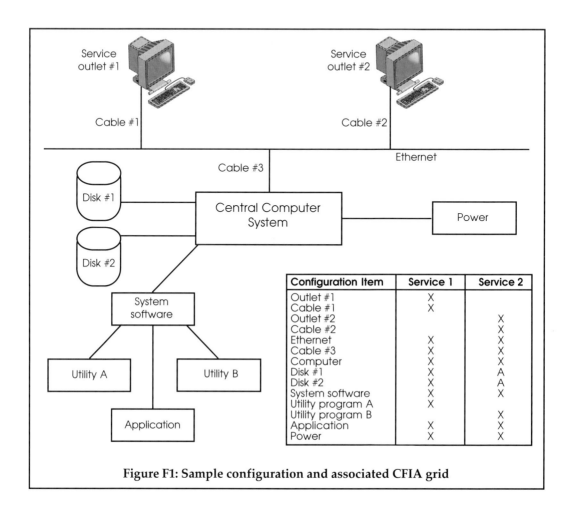

Configuration Item	Service 1	Service 2
Outlet #1	X	
Cable #1	X	
Outlet #2		X
Cable #2		X
Ethernet	X	X
Cable #3	X	X
Computer	X	X
Disk #1	X	A
Disk #2	X	A
System software	X	X
Utility program A	X	
Utility program B		X
Application	X	X
Power	X	X

Figure F1: Sample configuration and associated CFIA grid

F.2 Fault Tree Analysis

Fault Tree Analysis is a technique that can be used to determine the chain of events that causes a disruption of IT services. This technique, in conjunction with the calculation methods of Annex B, offers detailed models of availability. The main advantages of FTA are:

* FTA can be used for availability calculations

* operations can be performed on the resulting fault tree, these operations correspond with design options

* the desired level of detail in the analysis can be chosen.

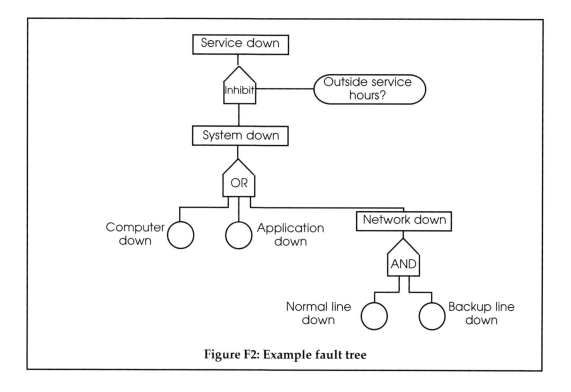

Figure F2: Example fault tree

FTA makes a representation of a chain of events using boolean notation. Figure F2 gives an example of a fault tree.

Essentially FTA distinguishes the following events.

* **basic events** - terminal points for the fault tree, eg power failure, operator error. Basic events are not investigated in greater depth. If basic events are investigated in further depth, they automatically become resulting events.

* **resulting events** - intermediate nodes in the fault tree resulting from a combination of events. The top most point in the fault tree is usually a failure of the IT service.

* **conditional events** - events that only occur under certain conditions, eg failure of the air-conditioning equipment only affects the IT service if equipment temperature exceeds the serviceable values.

* **trigger events** - events that trigger other events, eg power failure detection equipment can trigger automatic shutdown of IT services.

These events can be combined using logic operators, ie:

* **AND-gate** - the resulting event only occurs when all input events occur simultaneously. AND-gates correspond with the parallel chains in annex B.

* **OR-gate** - the resulting event occurs when one or more of the input events occurs. OR-gates correspond with the series chains in Annex B.

* **exclusive OR-gate** - the resulting event occurs when one and only one of the input events occurs.

* **inhibit gate** - the resulting event only occurs when the input condition is not met.

The mathematical evaluation of a fault tree is beyond the scope of this module, but can be found in the literature listed in the bibliography (Section 8).

Annex G. Designing for availability

G.1 Outline design process

This annex discusses the various technical issues involved in the design of new, and the modification of existing, IT services in order to meet availability requirements.

Availability should be considered in the design process (for both hardware and software) at the earliest possible stage, because it is always more costly to change the infrastructure used to provide the IT service after development has started. Participation of the Availability Manager in the design process can be divided into three tasks:

* specification of the availability requirements of hardware and software

* participation in infrastructure design regarding availability

* specification of component reliability and maintainability requirements and specification of serviceability requirements in the procurement documentation.

G.2 Service design availability analysis

The first stage is to understand the vulnerability to failure of the IT infrastructure. Suitable techniques are:

* Component Failure Impact Analysis (CFIA) - this identifies which configuration items are used by the service and helps to highlight areas where the availability can be improved cost effectively

* Failure Tree Analysis (FTA) - this provides a mathematical model of the system allowing prediction of availability from reliability, maintainability and serviceability estimates for each CI.

These techniques are outlined in Annex F.

G.3 Improving the design

The second stage is to improve the design if the availability requirements are not met. Various steps can be taken to improve the availability. Essentially they are:

* reduce the downtime per incident, ie improve maintainability

* reduce the number of incidents in a given period, ie improve reliability.

Concentrating on reducing the downtime, it is possible to:

* reduce the time between occurrence of the failure and actual detection of the failure, eg by using diagnostic tools, audiovisual alarms

* reduce the time between detection and diagnosis, eg by efficient incident control procedures

* reduce the time needed for diagnosis, eg by using diagnostic tools, testing environments

* reduce the time needed for repair, eg through modular design, clear documentation, implementation of temporary fixes, use of spare configuration items

* reduce the time needed for recovery, eg efficient backup/restore procedures, ability to retry operations, automatic recovery of database from journals

* reduce the overall time until restoration of the IT service, eg skill levels of staff, education and training, communication facilities among staff

* expedite engineer attendance!

To implement these techniques cost effectively, it is required that they are considered during design.

Reduction of the number of service failures can also be implemented in several ways:

* fault-tolerant techniques, ie permitting faults to occur in system components while eliminating the detrimental effects of faults

* duplexing or the provision of alternative system components to allow one system component to take over the work of another system component

* using more reliable components, eg by testing system components against specified requirements

* screening of new system components, ie operating new system components in an isolated environment to detect and repair early faults

* using self-testing components.

IT services are generally delivered by an infrastructure consisting of a number of elements, each contributing to the overall availability. Typically the factors that influence availability include:

* central hardware (see section G.4)

* local hardware (see section G.5)

* networks (see section G.6)

* environment (see section G.7)

* system software (see section G.8)

* applications software (see section G.9)

* operational standards, procedures and training (see section G.10)

* contracts with suppliers (see section G.11).

The following subsections deal with issues concerning the impact on availability of each of these factors. Note that the Availability Manager cannot be expected to be an expert on all of these matters.

G.4   Central hardware

Equipment selection

Detection of faults and potential failures has become one of the prime concerns of central hardware equipment suppliers.

Transient faults are likely to occur, especially within electronic systems. Methods to contain such faults employed in hardware such as error-correcting memory or disk, are important.

The ability to detect and retry a failing operation can increase effective reliability. This may be achieved by a combination of hardware and operating system functions.

It is useful to stipulate such features as mandatory requirements in the procurement process, if the availability requirements demand high reliability.

Configuration

The following techniques are commonly used to improve the availability of a central hardware system in the presence of a faulty component:

* some components may not, or can be designed not to, form part of the minimum infrastructure needed to run the service. This is the case for general support such as optional printers, disks or tape drives

* the service may be designed to operate for some hours without an item, for example, the audit trail might be redirected to disk if there are no operational tape drives

* a degraded but sufficient service may be offered on a reduced configuration, ie with less main memory, one CPU instead of two, fewer disk-controllers and hence, less throughput to the disks. This requires a trade-off between availability and performance, but is only an option when the performance degradation is acceptable

* extra equipment may be switched in from other, less important services running from the same centre or from a spare pool, eg a software development service that uses a similar processor.

Although these techniques can sustain IT service operation through the point of failure, some of the above will involve a system stop and restart, though this depends on the operating system capabilities. The resulting recovery time may not be acceptable and alternative methods may need to be adopted. Disk failures are typically the most time consuming failure from which to recover from and are also a likely major component to fail.

To solve this problem, a number of operating systems can now provide for two identical copies of a disk to be kept, with restart being possible from the non-failing copy. This is termed duplex disk operation or mirrored disks. It is a software rather than a hardware feature and requires extra hardware and thus extra cost in that two disks are needed for the storage capacity of one disk. This technique also affects the performance of the duplexed disk system either for better or for worse, depending on the operating system capabilities. Care must be taken to allow for the recovery overhead of the duplex disk system after a failing disk has been repaired or replaced.

Fault tolerance

To go beyond the level where an adequate service can be provided by fast restarts, an infrastructure capable of tolerating or absorbing applicable categories of fault is required, with this ability covering all the key components. Such an infrastructure will almost inevitably involve some form of duplexed disks and at least two of all other critical peripherals. In addition the key electronic components, particularly the processor, memory and communication channels to input/output devices, will also need to be duplicated. There must be at least two of each such key components in the system for continued operation to be possible.

There are two main options giving the ability to continue to provide the required service through hardware faults.

* The first option is to employ a combination of fault-detecting hardware and operating system to enable any activity in progress in a failing item to be redone or restarted on the remaining configuration. This is a fault-tolerant technique, when the operation does not perceivably affect the service

* The second option is to provide multiple processing paths and to compare results, accepting the result of the majority of the paths. This fully absorbs a failure.

If the availability requirements are not stringent enough to require fault-tolerant techniques, it may be acceptable to use relatively less reliable components but to duplicate them. Alternatively it may be more cost effective to use unreplicated components of greater reliability.

Repair and recovery time

Central hardware components are moving from a position where failures of individual components were a regular occurrence, but then were often repairable on-site, to a position where failures are less frequent, but repair takes longer as a replacement has to be delivered or complex repair procedures have to be followed.

Remote diagnostics

As reliability improves suppliers are improving the power of diagnostic software. The latter is designed to identify and report component failure. When the software is linked direct to the maintenance supplier, (ie remote diagnostics) replacement parts can be dispatched immediately. Replacement can then be performed more quickly by:

* an engineer who travels directly to the site

* an operator (in the case of some hardware).

Swift detection of faults and remote diagnostics can dramatically reduce the amount of downtime and is very effective where levels of high availability are required. Security needs to be carefully considered, especially regarding confidentiality and integrity.

G.5 Local hardware

The term local hardware applies to configuration items that are placed in customers' offices or otherwise geographically distributed. The failure of one item does not necessarily impinge on the service provided to customers. Local hardware includes local printers, terminals and PCs.

Modelling availability can become quite difficult for remote sites. The formulae in Annex B (Example 2) provide the basis for calculating availability. Because of the nature of remote sites, it involves networks which make the calculations more complicated. By making the calculations stage by stage the calculation process is simplified.

Local hardware is characterized by:

* low cost on an individual component basis

* being limited in respect to features to monitor and improve reliability and maintainability.

Local hardware is usually supplied on an 'as is' basis. Therefore, it is difficult, if not impossible, to increase the fault handling or recovery ability of any individual unit. Hence, the required level of service must be sought in numbers, eg spare units, and not by individual adjustments or changes.

Different network configurations may improve service availability. If required, networks should be configured for resilience to improve availability, ie build in some redundancy.

Local computers

There is often a distinguishing feature present in the availability requirements placed on local computers, as compared to the central system. The central system serves all customers, whereas the local hardware serves only the customers at that site. Therefore, there is the possibility of looking at local systems and services on a site-by-site basis. It is likely that the requirements vary between sites, even within the same service, and that this is not always fully considered when availability requirements are specified on an overall basis.

Geography

A key determinant of overall downtime is the time needed for spares to arrive on site, although remote diagnostics may help considerably here. Problems of geography must be taken into account if IT services are rendered on multiple, geographically separated sites. Appropriate potential suppliers must be assessed as to their nearest capable establishment.

Arrangements might be required to allow simple repairs to be made by qualified staff at the remote sites.

However, the key distinction will be between those items where there are more than one on the site and those that are unique. For the former the question will be whether there are enough, or whether one (or more) needs to be provided for resilience as a spare. For the latter, the first question will need to be whether this uniqueness is necessary. Are there alternatives that allow continued functioning in the event of a failure?

Key factors

The key factors to consider are:

* user maintenance, eg can the user or other non-IT skilled staff diagnose and repair faults

* the relative criticality of the service to the user population at the site both generally and for key services

* the availability of alternative or similar hardware close by, generally and for key services

* the locations of the supplier service representatives and spares depot

* the expected reliability and maintainability of each component and the effect of failure to the IT service of each component.

The following additional factors apply when considering availability of remote hardware:

* the potential for accidental damage induced by customers, which is not usually covered by any supplier warranty

* the heavy mechanical usage of low-cost items such as keyboards and terminal printers

* the relative skill and competence of suppliers' staff sent to service low-cost remote devices, compared with those dealing with the central system and its attached devices

> * the difficulty end-users face in providing sufficient information to support staff to diagnose the failing configuration item correctly, and thus, the potential for false call-outs to maintenance suppliers.

Remote sites

To overcome these problems the use of remote diagnostics may be of benefit. It will be particularly helpful where staff at remote sites are able to replace system components (some suppliers advocate this practice on major items like processor boards, disk-drives and even power packs).

Dispatch of a replacement by courier from the supplier's premises may be triggered by self diagnostic hardware. Replacement on site can subsequently be performed by operational staff. Care should be taken that the appropriate problem and change control procedures are observed so that warranties etc. are not invalidated.

Other methods that might be employed to improve the availability of remote hardware include:

> * holding a spare terminal or printer at a key site which can be swapped with a failing unit by the local staff provided they have the correct instructions and training and are not placed in any danger (either electrical or mechanical)
>
> * connecting adjacent terminals via different paths, including cables, controllers and network links, back to the centre, thus losing only a proportion after a failure
>
> * providing facilities to redirect printer output to alternative printers and allow the use of alternative terminals
>
> * specifying the procurement of more reliable equipment, which is usually more expensive. Extensive evaluation of functionally similar remote hardware, but from different suppliers, should take place before large quantities are ordered to assist in equipment selection and to support evidence of design MTBFs.

G.6 Networks

Network strategy and network design are the key determinants in network availability. It must be noted that both network strategy and design are outside the scope of the availability management function. Like performance management, network design might place constraints on the availability management function which limit the ability of the Availability Manager to commit to high availability. See the IT Infrastructure Library module on **Network Management** for guidance on network strategies.

Networks can include combinations of the following:

* modems, protocol converters and multiplexers

* communications processors

* communications software

* digital or analogue leased lines

* satellite, microwave and cellular radio connections

* communications interfaces in computers and terminals

* cabling infrastructure (passive and active components).

Whatever the complexity of the network, the prime factors affecting availability of network components and hence the network remain the same for all networks. These are given below together with the network components affected and some typical effects:

* line quality; this can be due to low or varying transmission quality, interference or cross-talk and can affect the public switched telephone network (PSTN), analogue or digital leased lines, LAN cabling, satellite links, cellular or microwave radio. The effects include partial loss or fluctuating levels of service, or even total loss of service. Typical remedies include error detection and retry, use of alternative transmission speeds, use of alternative paths, use of greater bandwidth or a mixture of several methods

* wear-and-tear; this affects most components, especially those with moving and mechanical parts, and is usually preceded by a period of increasing error rates, which may be detected by monitoring

* damage; all components, including the lines themselves, can be damaged. Damage may result in a total loss of service, which may take an extended period of time to repair. Typical remedies include the use of alternative paths, as well as keeping spare cables and connectors to hand. Some preventive

measures can be taken for common causes of
damage, such as preventing the build up of
electrostatic charges, secure mounting of network
equipment, fastening of connectors, using tamper-
proof connections and network equipment.

These factors can trigger secondary factors such as:

* overloading caused by high error rates or high traffic
  levels from re-routed data

* incorrect procedures caused by unanticipated error
  situations.

Typical network
availabilities

Most suppliers of communications equipment will, if
pressed, give some indication of the expected reliability of
their equipment. For communications equipment this is
usually expressed in terms of the mean time between
failures (MTBF). Maintenance agreements typically quote
an expected average time to repair and a target call out time
within which the service engineer is expected to arrive on
site. This data is insufficient to calculate the actual
availability, since the total time from failure to recovery is
needed.

For local area networks, rented lines or network services
(such as British Telecom's Global Network Services (GNS)
incorporating Packet Switch-Stream (PSS) services)
availability values are not usually quoted although there
are some indications that this may change in the future. The
network designers must therefore rely in part on their own
estimates of availability based upon past experience and
measurements or the experience of existing customers in
order to predict the level of availability.

G.7 Environment

This is the element of the IT infrastructure over which there
is least control but upon which greatest reliance tends to be
placed. Careful analysis of failures should reveal the effect
of many unusual incidents whether it be the unexpected
cutting off of the main power supply during a 'practice' fire
drill or perhaps eating of cables by rodents.

The effect of some environmental failures may invoke the
implementation of contingency plans. Some measures taken
by the Availability Manager can actually prevent some
contingencies.

The principal environmental elements which affect availability are:

* electrical power

* temperature and humidity

* building and ergonomic design

* other environmental influences, such as dust, fire, flooding, vibrations.

Electrical power

The increasing usage of, and resulting dependency on, on-line services and terminals means that to maintain the IT services requires that power must be provided to more than just a central computer. Terminals, for example, are usually connected directly to the normal mains power sockets and so the provision of special feeds may not be practical. To continue to work in the presence of a power cut may therefore require not only that the central computer itself has standby power but that so do designated areas. This also applies to remote hardware and network equipment in geographically separated areas. The same argument applies to temperature and lighting equipment.

A number of sites are finding that even when the power is available it is not satisfactory. In offices, especially older ones, the power supply and wiring are being called upon to support other electrical equipment, including terminals, which can lead to lowered voltages, spikes and transients from high power (using) devices such as photocopiers and kettles. Greenfield sites may be no better; one organization on an industrial estate found induced interference and breaks caused by building work, a major problem.

Since the technical evaluation of power problems and the design of specific remedies is likely to be beyond the capability of the IT staff, specialist advice will need to be sought. The specialists must be given a clear idea of the availability requirement and, probably from the supplier, the power requirements of the IT equipment. Detailed discussions and the analysis of options will be required when the availability requirements of the customer or the power requirements of the IT equipment change.

Techniques to improve IT service availability in the presence of power faults are:

* improve the power provision by using the following techniques which are in order of increasing cost

  - filtering of the power to remove transients and, with some equipment, temporary low voltage conditions

  - use of an alternator to smooth the power and in some cases override a short power cut

  - provision of a generator, enabling power to be restored within a few minutes of a cut

  - an uninterruptible power supply (UPS) system providing clean power regardless of the mains power state.

* use a computer system which has enough battery power to retain memory contents and processor state, enabling continuation if power returns within a few minutes

* design the system to effect a fast recovery after a detected power fault.

Temperature and humidity control

There is a need to keep all the electronic equipment, necessary to provide a service, operating within the correct bands of temperature and humidity. In the case of mainframes the correct levels are usually more stringent than the levels for other electronic equipment. Even when the service is not running, it will be necessary to maintain the same control to prevent condensation inside the equipment.

When these limits cannot be maintained it may be necessary to shut down the service. This is for two main reasons. Firstly, there may be a real risk of damage not just to one item, but to the whole configuration and secondly, continued operation could invalidate the maintenance agreement. Just repairing the air conditioning is not sufficient; it is necessary to wait until the temperature and humidity return to acceptable levels. Time must also be allowed for the hardware to acclimatize and reach an operational temperature. The length of time this will take is unpredictable.

Within offices a gradually increasing amount of electronic equipment, all generating heat, may overwhelm the cooling capabilities, whether this is provided by air conditioning or natural ventilation. Particularly in sealed buildings, the original air conditioning may not be powerful enough to cope. Equipment that is subjected to frequent high temperatures may not immediately fail but will become increasingly unreliable.

The main requirement to assure adequate reliability is to size the heat load accurately, both initially and as more computer equipment is added, and then to ensure that the anticipated availability of the cooling plant is factored into the overall IT service figures.

Figures for typical intervals between failures and for repair times are available for such plants from suppliers. The engineers responsible for designing the plant should be involved in the initial assessment and be asked to provide anticipated figures before the plant design is finalized. Simple things can assist, such as using three slightly smaller air conditioners instead of two, giving a greater resilience when one fails.

The IT Infrastructure Library Environmental Modules as described in section 2.5, should be consulted for further information and also the module on **Computer Installation & Acceptance**.

Building design and ergonomic factors

Although building specification and building design is outside the scope of the availability management function, building design can limit or modify the options which exist to match availability requirements.

A frequent cause of failure is the accidental knocking over of equipment or the accidental pressing of buttons. Ergonomic design can assist in the prevention of such failures. Measures include stable and secure placement of equipment and protective caps over controls that should not normally be used.

Ergonomic design can also reduce downtime by reducing the time needed for diagnosis and repair. Measures include colour coding of cables, adequate lighting conditions (especially in otherwise unmanned areas) and the height at which equipment controls are located. Maintenance contracts with suppliers may require that several rules regarding service clearance, ie adequate room for the maintenance engineer to work in, are observed.

Other environmental factors

Many other environmental factors may cause damage to and failure of computer equipment. Some factors may cause damage beyond a level that can be repaired within the agreed terms in the Service Level Agreement. In that case a Contingency Plan will have to be invoked. Other factors just cause service breaks.

The most notable factors are:

* dust or particle density

  high dust levels can cause unreliability. Disk drives
  are especially sensitive to this. Measures to reduce
  dust levels include air locks, non-smoking policy,
  air-intake filters, regular cleaning, separating dust
  sensitive equipment (such as non-sealed disk drives)
  from dust producing equipment (printers)

* electrical interference

  equipment may fail or even be damaged by
  electrostatic charges and electromagnetic fields.
  Appropriate earthing of equipment is essential, as
  well as using materials that allow electrostatic
  charges to leak away. Where there are intense,
  external electromagnetic fields problems may occur
  if the building is not properly shielded, eg near high
  voltage power lines, powerful radio transmitters

* vibrations

  low frequency vibrations of the building due to
  nearby motorways, railways, building work and
  heavy machinery may cause failure in computer
  equipment, especially to sensitive electromechanical
  equipment, such as disk drives, but also to other
  equipment by causing printed circuit board breaks or
  loose connections. Such equipment may be shielded
  from vibrations by placing them on shock absorbing
  pedestals or floors.

Other influences include fire, flood, rodent or insect
infestations, radiation levels and density of airborne toxic
substances.

G.8   System software

Controlling availability of system software components is
not an easy task. The availability management function
must ensure that:

* the reliability of the system software is ascertained
  (eg from the experience and satisfaction of customers
  elsewhere)

* the relationship between the system software
  supplier and the hardware supplier, where they are
  different, is stable and that there is satisfactory
  acceptance of the relationship by a number of
  existing customers

    *   it is always possible to back out changes to system software and revert to the previous version

    *   necessary patches and other fixes to the system software are implemented speedily, but not without the proper controls

    *   security mechanisms controlling access to system software are adequate.

Special controls are needed for those system software components that require customization to the organization's needs, because failures caused by errors in these components are not usually covered by maintenance agreements.

In the case of high availability requirements where more than one processor is needed there is a design requirement to ensure that system software resides in all processors and is kept in step. This should be mandatory where operating systems help to ensure availability by managing hardware and software processes as well as keeping backups ready for immediate takeover in the event of the detection of an error.

Making sure that the computer operations staff, their support staff and customers are well trained will go a long way to ensuring that unavailability of a system due to system software faults is kept low. Refer to the IT Infrastructure Library module on **Software Control & Distribution** for related guidance.

G.9 Application software and data

Techniques to improve the reliability and maintainability of application software apply to both in-house developed software and third party software, although the form of measures taken are usually different. Third party software and its maintenance is largely covered in contractual agreement, ie serviceability criteria, whereas the reliability and maintainability of in-house developed software is usually agreed with application development groups within the IT Directorate.

Although design of application software is outside the scope of the availability management function there are several factors to be taken into consideration concerning the reliability and maintainability of application software. Measures that can be taken to reduce the downtime caused by application faults are:

* comprehensive testing of code before going live

* software verification and data validation techniques within the application software, allowing swift detection and prevention of faults

* concise, clear error messages that pinpoint the location and reason for failure to aid diagnosis

* modular software design methods reducing both the complexity of diagnosis and the possibly detrimental side-effects of repair

* clear application documentation and documented code to aid repairs

* documentation of recent changes

* agreements with application development or maintenance groups and third party suppliers on call-out and fix times for necessary maintenance

* automated code generation to avoid coding errors.

Much can be done to reduce the time needed for recovery and restoration of the IT service after a failure, whether resulting from the application itself or from the infrastructure elements on which the application runs. Some techniques, especially those suitable for high availability, need to be taken into account during the design of the application software. Techniques include:

* backup and restore procedures for the application data, especially regarding frequency and content of backups. When a continuous service is provided, care must be taken that the software allows a backup to be made of sufficient integrity to provide easy restoration of the data. When very high availability is required it may be necessary to retain the last backup on online high speed devices, such as spare disks

* transaction logging to recover changes to the data made since the last backup

* checkpoints in online and batch transactions to facilitate rollback so that only the work since the last checkpoint needs to be rerun

* before and after image journals of changes made to data to ensure integrity of the data and the database

* the use of logical access mechanisms to enable recovery on other system elements than the original ones, allowing faulty components to be repaired while the service continues, eg preventing the "hard-coding" of device names

* parallel or "shadow" operation on different infrastructure elements to provide a complete take-over in the event of failure.

Steps can also be taken to improve the reliability of application software, such as:

* testing software; this topic is discussed in the IT Infrastructure Library module on **Testing Software for Operational Use**

* the use of structured software design methods, such as SSADM (Structured System Analysis and Design Method)

* various quality techniques, such as walkthroughs, design reviews and formal Quality Assurance procedures

* the use of fault-tolerant techniques in application software.

When software is purchased from third party suppliers, make sure that the supplier has a satisfactory track record in supporting products after delivery. Key factors to consider are:

* stability of the supplier

* maintenance record of the supplier

* version/release policy used by the supplier

* amount of support given to sold product.

G.10 Operational standards, procedures and training

All factors that influence availability covered in this annex need a high level of training for all the infrastructure and service support staff involved. In fact the higher the availability required the more important training becomes. In the event of a failure operational staff are under pressure to act quickly and accurately. The pressure increases for higher levels of required availability.

Availability can also be improved by considering organizational standards and procedures. Standards and procedures must fit the design criteria regarding availability. Key factors influencing availability in this area are the:

* presence of support staff; this applies especially to IT services that have service hours outside normal office hours

* ability to contact key support staff; IT services requiring high availability may require paging devices or portable telephones for key support staff

* modification procedures; steps must be taken to ensure that changes to the infrastructure that can cause downtime are tested and implemented outside service hours

* efficiency of Help Desk call handling, escalation and problem control procedures.

Failures will need to be contained to reduce the impact on customers. On each occurrence of a failure an agreed plan should be followed to ensure the least amount of disruption for the customers.

For each failure that involves contact with suppliers the Availability Manager must be satisfied that:

* the failure is timed and documented

* the documentation is accurate

* the contractual serviceability criteria applicable to the suppliers' contracts are monitored, eg when a contract specifies that a service engineer should be on the premises within two hours after the first call, this should be monitored

* actions taken following failures both by external and internal staff are correct

* the appropriate penalty clauses from a contract are invoked when a supplier does not comply with the serviceability criteria in the contract

* incidents are escalated to appropriate levels both within IT services and by the contractor

* affected customers are informed of the progress made in the resolution of the incident

        * steps are taken after each incident to ensure that similar incident(s) do not recur.

Note that some of these points are outside the control of the availability management function.

G.11 Contracts with suppliers

The Availability Manager oversees the contractual serviceability of supplied systems.

In specifying the serviceability requirements for a suitable maintenance contract with a supplier the Availability Manager's main objective is to ensure that the service(s) provided to the customer conform(s) to the requirements as documented in the SLAs.

Procedures and systems are required to:

    * give details on the contractual serviceability requirements for each supplier

    * establish measurements to monitor the performance of the contractor against the agreed requirements

    * ensure procedures and systems are in place to monitor whether the contractors' requirements on the IT Services section are being met.

In some instances suppliers may not include scheduled downtimes in failure statistics and measurements for contractual purposes. Where services are required 24 hours a day, 7 days a week, scheduled maintenance services and modifications must be performed on non-operational units.

Note that serviceability as contractually agreed with suppliers covers only partially the availability of IT services as perceived by the end-user (see also Annex E).

Annex H. Data items to be recorded for each incident

The following list contains the minimum data items that need to be recorded to monitor compliance to Service Level Agreements and supplier compliance to contractual serviceability criteria:

* date and time at which the incident occurs

* date and time at which the incident is reported

* date and time at which the incident is resolved

* failing configuration item

* date and time at which the supplier is notified

* date and time supplier reported the failing item to be repaired

* date and time at which recovery action is initiated

* date and time at which the service is restored.

CCTA hopes that you find this book both useful and interesting. We will welcome your comments and suggestions for improving it.
Please use this form or a photocopy, and continue on a further sheet if needed.

From:

Name

Organization

Address

Telephone

COVERAGE
Does the material cover your needs?
If not, then what additional material would you like included.

CLARITY
Are there any points which are unclear?
If yes, please detail where and why.

ACCURACY
Please give details of any inaccuracies found.

If more space is required for these or other comments, please continue overleaf.

OTHER COMMENTS

Return to: **CCTA Library**
               Rosebery Court
               St Andrews Business Park
               NORWICH, NR7 0HS

Further information

Further information on the contents of this module can be obtained from:

CCTA Library
Rosebery Court
St Andrews Business Park
NORWICH
NR7 0HS.

Telephone: 01603 704 930
GTN: 3040 4930

Printed in the United Kingdom for The Stationery Office
TJ002146 7/00 C6 10170